1976

BETWEEN

SURVIVAL

AND

SUICIDE

BETWEEN SURVIVAL AND SUICIDE

EDITOR

BENJAMIN B. WOLMAN
Long Island University

CONSULTING EDITOR

HERBERT H. KRAUSS
Hunter College

GARDNER PRESS, INC.

NEW YORK

*Distributed by Halsted Press
Division of John Wiley & Sons, Inc.*

NEW YORK • TORONTO • LONDON • SYDNEY

Gardner Press, Inc.
32 Washington Square West
New York, New York 10011

Distributed Solely by the Halsted Press Division
of John Wiley & Sons, Inc., New York.

Library of Congress Cataloging in Publication Data

Between survival and suicide.

CONTENTS: Boss, M. Flight from death (mere survival).—Krauss, H.H. Suicide: a sociological and psychological phenomenon.—Lifton, R.J. On death and the continuity of life. (etc.)
1. Suicide—Addresses, essays, lectures. I. Wolman, Benjamin B.

HV6545.B43   362.2   75-17706
ISBN 0-470-95944-4

CONTENTS

BETWEEN

SURVIVAL

AND

SUICIDE

PREFACE

The tragedy of self-inflicted death has always attracted the attention of philosophers and theologians, but the scholarly analysis of suicide has but a short history. Suicide is by no means a simple issue, for it hinges on a variety of psychological, sociological, ethical, and legal problems and no one has so far offered an equivocal and satisfactory answer to all the questions raised by this perplexing phenomenon.

The questions one must ask are complex and diversified. Assuming that all living organisms fight for survival, what is then the cause of suicide? Why do certain countries in certain times have a high incidence of suicide cases? Can the differences in suicide rates be explained by differences in age, sex, race, religion, culture, climate, or social system? Is suicide a psychological or sociological phenomenon? Is suicide psychologically "normal" or is it a symptom of a mental disorder? What are the ethical, philosophical, legal, and religious implications of suicide? And, finally, does an individual have the right to put an end to his own life?

The eight Contributors to this volume address themselves to these problems and to a score of other relevant issues. No editorial effort was made to attain any consensus of opinion, and the choice of contributors was based on their intellectual acumen and moral independence.

The issues at stake are vital, thus the polemic must be vigorous. The aim of this volume is to stimulate discussion rather than stifle it, and its spirit is thought-provoking rather than didactic or hortatory.

The present volume bears witness to the widespread differences of opinion on a diversity of approaches to the problem of suicide.

I have made no effort to reconcile the views of the contributors, nor have I tried to mollify their tone and style. These eight essays were written by independent authors, who are expressing their original views in a frank and intellectually stimulating manner.

The issues discussed in this volume are controversial. So are the eight essays.

B.B. Wolman

I want to express my profound gratitude to Professor Herbert H. Krauss, who as Consulting Editor greatly helped me in the selection of authors and in reading their manuscripts.

B. B. W.

I

Flight From Death—Mere Survival; and Flight Into Death—Suicide

MEDARD BOSS

FLIGHT FROM DEATH AND FLIGHT INTO DEATH SEEM TO BE TWO diametrically opposed modes of human behavior. Appearances are deceptive, however, for flight from death and flight into death are different ways of fleeing from one and the same thing. In both, the full unfolding of human existence is evaded. The difference is more quantitative than qualitative.

Such insight is only possible when we clarify the nature of human living as well as the character of human dying. Only then can we understand the motives which induce one person to flee from death and into the state of mere survival of a day-to-day existence, and another to flee from life and into the death of a suicide.

Unfortunately, physicians, who have most to do with human living and dying, and who should be best informed, are for the most part uninformed about the conditions under which most people live and die. This is because their medical training focuses on the existing yet mortal human being. Medical students are first instructed in physics, chemistry, and zoology. The human being is, however, neither nonliving material, nor a mere plant or animal. It is certainly possible to gather a great deal of useful and necessary information about man by studying the natural sciences; but although this information leads directly to the astonishing therapeutic success of somatic medicine, that which is specifically human about human existence remains obscure. The methods of investigation of the natural sciences do not even touch the realm of human phenomena, let alone elucidate it. For example, all the discoveries of brain physiology and molecular biology contribute nothing to an understanding of human consciousness. The relationship of these discoveries to the phenomena of human perception of what is real and meaningful, is never more than a relationship of when and then. *When* I look out of a darkened room at the brilliant sun and perceive it as the brilliant sun, *then* it is possible, with the aid of an electroencephalogram, to detect electrical currents. The attempt to establish a causal relationship between the two, to say that the brain processes produce my understanding of the sun *as* the sun, or that they are the substrate or basis of this understanding, is nothing more than magical thinking under the guise of science. It is not possible to think meaningfully in terms of such a relationship between so-called somatic processes and a so-called psyche.

If the information gained from the natural sciences does not lead to the slightest understanding of the humanness of human existence, neither can it lead to an understanding of the ending of human existence, which is death. At most, the natural sciences can formulate the death of the human being as an analogy to the ending of a lifeless thing. Medicine, founded on the natural sciences, can understand death as the failure to appear of a last component of a present thing—a component, due to arrive at some later time, that is similar to the last installment of a monetary debt. Other concrete things that are accessible to the natural sciences end in other ways. The rain comes to an end; it has disappeared; it stops. The path ends; it stops, complete or incomplete. A machine comes to the end of its functioning, a cogwheel is broken.

The death of the human being, however, cannot be appropriately characterized in any of these terms. None of these ways of ending is comparable with the dying of the human being. The ending of human life may be compared to the ripening of a fruit, but even in these terms, appearances are deceptive. Certainly the still unripe fruit, and likewise the still living human being, carry their own completion and perfection in themselves insofar as they are able, in the course of their lives, to become that which they are not yet. Just as with the unripe fruit, the dasein of the human being is always its "not-yet," a "not-yet" that like their own possibilities belongs to them from the beginning. The fruit, however, reaches perfection when it is ripe. Most human beings die mostly before they have reached their own perfection, or else they die used up, and in a state of decay. It is also clear that botany cannot elucidate the death of the human being. Man exists and dies in a way that only he can.

It follows, then, that from the very outset the concepts of the natural sciences prove inadequate to conceptualize human existence as well as human dying. Neither the one nor the other can be conceptually understood, as long as "concept" is understood in the sense of modern science. A conceptualized "concept," as such, is reached through a definition. Since antiquity, a definition has meant: "*fit per genus proximum et differentiam specificam.*" Neither death nor life can be categorized in this way. Our modern concepts are therefore totally inadequate to deal with them.

In passing, it is worth pointing out that our modern concepts and conceptions are generally inadequate when it comes to fundamental things. The fundamental given things, the realities that enable us to exist as we are, cannot be conceptually grasped, let alone scientifically proven. Science has to accept the fundamental things just as given objects, in order to be able to process them in accord with its nature as "natural science." Its inadequacy to produce a conceptual understanding of space or of the nature of space is just as profound as its inadequacy in the case of life and death. It is possible to work out a scientific concept of space by attributing a homogeneity to space and then measuring it. However, it is only possible to attribute a characteristic to something, and so to measure it, when that something is already present, already given. A different method of investigation is necessary to elucidate the fundamental character of this already present and given something, and then to show what underlying characteristics exist within this character that make it what it is. Such a method has to be appropriate to the special character of what is to be investigated.

It is, then, not possible to clarify the nature of human existence and dying if we simply, without reflection, apply a method which has proven itself only in investigating nonliving things. Human living and dying have to be investigated with a method that consists of nothing more than an unprejudiced, careful viewing or looking. A radical exclusion of all deriving, explaining, concluding, of hypothesis formation and calculated intervention is necessary. Human existence and dying are immediately accessible to a simple phenomenological way of study. The simple fact that we are capable of such study, so that by looking we are able to perceive and understand, shows us one of the fundamental features of our existence, common only to living things. Just as we are able to understand our own living and dying, so do we, as existing human beings, exist with the ability to perceive and respond to the meaningfulness of everything that we encounter in our world.

The ability to perceive and respond is not a function primarily encased in a psyche capsule or a defined consciousness, so that we have to reach out to the things in our world in some undiscovered way. We do not have to "transcend" these things; but as this ability to perceive and respond to whatever we encounter is fundamental to our perception of something as something, it can address us and therefore claim us. Had we not already developed the ability to perceive and respond to things that are, we could never grasp something and comprehend it. It is well known that one can only take hold of and grasp something when one is already by it. Because we have, by our basic nature, a world-spanning ability to perceive what we encounter, we are always in relation to what is encountered; always related to it, and always behaving toward it in this or that way. We are, first, in a perceiving relation to what is encountered.

That which is encountered then demands that we behave toward it in a way corresponding to its meaningfulness as it appears to us.

When we see ourselves as existing in this way as beings which possess the ability to behave in certain ways toward what is encountered, then it becomes clear that we are not present in the world as lifeless things. Such things can be adequately characterized by defining their presence and position in the pre-existing hollow space of a world. Furthermore, they claim and fill a space corresponding to their volume, and are at fixed calculable distances from other things. It is also possible to describe, with the physical senses, certain properties of these lifeless things. There is no trace of such properties to be found in the existence of the human being. The human being does not exist as some concrete present thing in itself with visible properties; rather, he exists as the unique totality of behavioral possibilities which he is able to live out, depending on which beings he encounters and which address themselves to him. We can say that our existence consists of our given possibilities for behaving toward whatever claims us or to whatever addresses itself to us. One can say that a tree trunk possesses the possibility of being made into a table by a carpenter, but then the tree trunk no longer has the possibility of being made into more tables. On the other hand, when a human being lives out one of his possibilities for behaving toward what he encounters, the possibility does not get used up; rather it comes to correspond to the meaningfulness of what is encountered, and therefore becomes more perfect and more practiced.

Among the diversity of human possibilities for behaving and existing, a careful scrutiny will reveal one that differs from all others in a unique way—that possibility of dying. This possibility of dying is so characteristic that human beings have been designated by it since the time of Parmenides—that is, as mortals. The possibility of dying is a distinguishing mark of human existence because it is extreme and cannot be bypassed. Its fulfillment, something which each of us must carry out, consists of our existence abandoning us.

The death of the human being is the possibility of being no longer dasein. It must be pointed out, that this existence possibility *is* a possibility of existing, and as such belongs to our fundamental nature. This means that it belongs to our existing and, to be sure, from the very beginning. As existing human beings, we consist, together with all other possibilities of behaving towards what encounters us, of this last possibility. This possibility of dying is already present as a possibility as the human being comes into life. As soon as the dasein exists, it is cast into the possibility of dying. The human being cannot comprehend this most authentic, most extreme, unavoidable possibility of living in the course of his existence. In dying, the dasein is confronted with itself in its most proper ability to be. Each human being has to die his own death. For the countless other possibilities of behaving, we can appoint a proxy; in dying, none of us is interchangeable.

The human being is aware of this most authentic and extreme possibility of dying as the most certain of all his possibilities. He perceives it as his being mortal. The human being is presumably the only living creature that knows with certainty of his being mortal, that he must die. As a result he is inevitably compelled somehow to take account of what he has perceived of it. He cannot do otherwise. One cannot simply not behave toward something that has once been perceived and known. For this reason, and in this sense, human life can also be designated as a being-to-death. Whether animals know about their mortality is uncertain, because they cannot speak to us about it. If they do not know, then they cannot die as the human being dies. They merely come to an end.

The most free, and the most worthy, of the human modes of behavior toward one's own mortality consists of holding this authentic extreme and last possibility constantly before one's eyes. In this way there is no hint of defeatism. It is not a matter of staring fixedly at death, or of believing that life and living can be neglected. On the contrary! If we remain constantly aware of our own dying, then all the other precursory possibilities of living that belong to our existing receive their proper rank and import. Remaining aware of our mortality preserves us from clinging obstinately to some precursory possibility of living, and making it an absolute. For example, when we confront our mortality, collecting riches and possessions as an absolute, exclusive goal, or losing ourselves in everyday activities become ridiculous modes of behavior. By constantly keeping the fact of our having to die before us, we gain the freedom to allow our fellow human beings to exist as the human beings that they are meant to be. Last but not least, the precursory modes of behavior which we exhibit in our professions and toward our colleagues attain the proper dignity and meaningfulness that they deserve only when we become and remain aware of our mortality. Only then are we aware that each moment of our lives is unrecoverable and is therefore to be used. This, in turn, is only possible when we answer the appeal of whatever we encounter in accord with its meaningfulness, at the moment we encounter it, with the commitment of our whole being. Were we immortal, then we would miss nothing; we could make up all our omissions and negligences. Because human life is finite, each and every moment counts. It counts toward our fulfillment and our becoming free only when we commit ourselves to a behavior toward that which encounters us in accordance with the claims it makes on us. Guilt and indebtedness arise when we neglect such possibilities.

On the other hand, not even shrinking from death as a dissolution into an empty nothingness, or as the end of all things can lead us to a free and pragmatic awareness of our mortality. Only one thing is certain; that the dasein, after dying, is no longer in the world in the same way it was before dying. Such certainty, however, in no way excludes the possibility that death is the radical annihilation of everything that is feared when one anxiously contemplates dying. Dying may well mean a transformation of the dasein's "being-in-the-world" into a totally different way of being; a way of being that is in no way reminiscent of other types of human "being" that change into other modes. For example, the dreaming human being is unaware of the way he has disposed of his waking existence after he has ceased sleeping. In his awake state, he dwells in a world with others who are also awake, but which is quite different from the world that enveloped him while he dreamt. While he dreamt, he perceived his dreaming mode of existing as the only possible state of "being-in-the-world." In the same way, while awake, we consider our actual waking state as the only possible mode of being.

Those human beings who have reached the highest possible degree of maturity, who are free, composed, and joyously serene, perceive death as transformation and as an absolute change. Those who perceive death as the fulfillment of the possibilities which embrace on the dasein, perceive that which is not at the dasein's disposal. The dasein that has been able to unfold and free itself into a composed, joyous serenity perceives the phenomenon of death as part of an existence which is not closed off and perfect in itself. In accord with his own fundamental nature, this individual is able to perceive his death as a manifestation of his own finiteness. He therefore perceives death as an indication of his being human, and is constantly open to that which is not merely another finite being, but to all that lays claim to the worldly realm of perceiving meaningfulness. How and where could something *be*—that is, be *present*—if there were no realm of openness, no openness in itself, or no open realm of perceiving?

Flight from Death—Mere Survival

A way of behaving toward our authentic and most extreme possibility, a way that is open and worthy of the human being, is not in great demand in our modern industrial society. For in this society, life, like everything else, is seen as belonging to our world. What encounters us can only appear as a possibility for production and for increasing the concentration of power in our hands. As a result, most people are concerned with hanging onto life as a lasting possession. Death must be denied, insofar as that is possible.

All of us are familiar with the countless ways of trying to flee from death. Most people blind themselves to their own mortality and perceive death solely as the death of others. Death is a disagreeable event that from time to time happens to this person or that person. One avoids getting too close to his own mortality by imagining that although death occasionally occurs, and others die, he will not for a long time. Therefore, dying seems to be a mere transformation of a living thing into a lifeless material.

We also keep our distance from our mortality by investigating dying from a psychological point of view. Basically, these studies are not significant investigations of dying; rather, they describe the behavior of the living. But death can only be understood from a philosophical viewpoint, as the necessary consequence of human finiteness.

Most people cannot bear to face the possibility of their dying. They flee from death, in that they deny it. The most usual denial of death is some form of addiction. All forms of addiction mean that the addict falls a helpless prey to the substance of his addiction, and is often so engulfed by it that he lapses into insensibility. In this way, he lulls to sleep the knowledge of his own death.

At present, the most widespread form of addiction is not to alcohol or drugs, but to work. In this mania for work, we lose ourselves to the goods we produce, and in so doing, become a mere product alienated from our own selves. We merely survive and no longer exist in the sense that distinguishes human existence. We do not even notice that this mode of survival is the same as a partial suicide. Nevertheless, there is no doubt that human existence is truncated when it buries its most authentic possibility, its mortality, and flees from facing it.

The worst of it is, is that those who flee from a binding knowledge of their mortality and mutilate their proper and full existence to a mere vegetable survival, undertake their flight on their own initiative, after deciding that they want it. The thoughtless, nonreflective spirit which rules our modern society gathers up most of these people while they are still very young, and sweeps them into this flight from death without their knowing what happens to them or why. Consequently, the existing majority of human beings who have the desire to just survive are less than human in that they are lost to the urges and pressures of their surroundings. They do not reflect on what is most characteristic of their humanness. They vegetate, blindly obeying the directions of some professional or non-professional organization. As Georg Volk in *Vom Arzt and vom Kranken* points out, even doctors and biologists, who are supposed to be the experts responsible for matters of life and death, speak of death as if it were just the remnant of a western inefficiency.

The most grotesque attempts to deny that the human being is mortal are encountered in certain funeral homes. There the corpse is cosmetically made up, a cigarette is thrust into its mouth, and tape recorders play back recorded conversations made while the dead man was alive.

FLIGHT INTO DEATH—SUICIDE

Suicides, in the usual sense of the word, differ from the existential partial suicides, in that the partial suicide is the denial of being mortal, while the suicide is the full flight from complete existence. Suicides extend the mutilation of their dasein to encompass their bodyliness, and so carry their flight to the point of total annihilation. However, total suicide, or even attempted total suicide, is practically always preceded by an existential partial suicide. In this respect, it is a matter of indifference whether the attempt is serious or theatrical, whether the attempt fails by chance, or whether the potential suicide makes sure that his attempt will fail.

There is, however, an infinitely small number of human beings who are able to unfold their nature to its fullest extent and who are motivated to suicide solely out of consideration for their fellow men. This occasionally happens when a seriously ill person knows that he suffers from a chronic, hopeless, inevitably fatal illness, and is ready to relieve his relatives of an oppressive burden by killing himself. Apart from this rare exception, only those human beings who have already strangled their dasein, and forced it into unbearable straits by an existential partial suicide, flee from life into total death. Such an extreme partial suicide can be forced on a person through a defective upbringing, in which case it is a psychoneurotically determined existential mutilation, or a defective maturity.

The existential partial suicide, which practically always precedes a total suicide, consists of the person (whether young or old) seeing himself as robbed of the potential of carrying to fulfillment all of the fundamental possibilities of relating that make up his nature. For this reason, all investigations have reached the same conclusion, namely, that those who commit suicide, or even make a serious attempt, act out of a feeling of insecurity, of not being loved, of unbearable isolation from their fellow human beings. Such a state necessarily means an extreme partial suicide, because the human being exists in accordance with his very nature together with other human beings in a common world. Each existential isolation, then, destroys at least half of him.

In view of this, it is clear why Stengel, in *Suicide and Attempted Suicide,* could point out that most suicides and attempted suicides have an appellative function. Hofmann confirmed this on the basis of his studies of eighty patients who had been interned in the University Medical Clinic of Zurich for having attempted suicide. According to Hofmann, many suicides are a last desperate cry, made in the hope that the environment will free them of their unbearable isolation from their fellow human beings. Ringel was able to show the significant fact that nearly every suicide—that is, in the usual sense of a total suicide—as well as every serious suicide attempt is preceded by an existential partial suicide. Ringel called this existential partial suicide the "pre-suicidal syndrome." Nevertheless, he meant nothing more than that state of existing that has been reduced to only a few rudimentary possibilities of relating to fellow human beings.

The person who commits suicide radically annihilates his dasein in order to burst the constricting limits of his existence; but he chooses exactly the wrong means. He destroys the bodily structure of his existence, instead of striving for the redeeming expansion and fullness of his previously shattered relations to his world and fellow human beings. He does not only not strive for such freedom, but he actually robs himself of each and every future possibility of maturing by his total self-destruction. In this way he flees from carrying to fulfillment a fully unfolded dasein, but he merely does so more completely than the one who denies his being mortal, who runs from standing firm in the fact of his own mortality and so truncates his existence.

In this respect I will cite two pieces of especially vivid evidence. The American psychoanalyst, Hendin, provides the first. He investigated suicide in three Scandinavian countries which are geographical neighbours, and which are related through hundreds of years of common history, yet have markedly different suicide rates. In each of those countries, he investigated groups of 20-30 psychotic and nonpsychotic patients who had unsucessfully tried to kill themselves. He compared these people with normal people, who had never felt any wish to kill themselves.

According to Hendin's investigations, Denmark and Sweden have the highest suicide rates in Europe. These rates are three times that of Norway. This relationship remains stable when comparisons are made between country and city regions; between the three capital cities of Copenhagen, Stockholm, and Oslo; between age groups; the sexes; and married and unmarried people. There are 20 suicides yearly for every 100,000 inhabitants of Denmark and Sweden, and 7.5 suicides yearly for every 100,000 inhabitants of Norway. Insofar as it is possible to trace these rates back, Denmark has had the highest rate in Europe for about a hundred years. Norway has always had a low rate. In Sweden the rate has climbed from a low rate at the beginning of the century to its present high level.

The suicide rates in Switzerland, Austria, Germany, and Japan are similar to that of Denmark and Sweden. America has about half as many.

Hendin began his investigations in Denmark. It struck him immediately that his patients were clearly aware that their act was a burden on the conscience of their fellow human beings. It seemed that this was frequently an additional recognized or unrecognized motive for the suicide attempt. To arouse guilt feelings in another is a way of appealing to him, of punishing him. How do the Danes learn this way of behaving toward their fellow men? It seems to be an important factor in upbringing, for Danish mothers show their children how grieved and distressed they are by their "bad" or "mean" behavior. This is connected to a characteristic form of dealing with aggressive behavior. Danish children are brought up with much leniency and kindness, but are not allowed to behave aggressively. Without hardness and firm discipline, but with a gentle guidance through the arousal of guilt feelings, they learn to behave in a "civilized" way. (In comparison with Danish children, American children seem like monsters.) A sense of humor, and joy in harmless teasing are two of the ways of living out aggressive tensions. This alone does not explain the high suicide rate. The English just as sternly forbid their children to behave aggressively, but have a low murder rate, as well as a low suicide rate.

The Danish form of depression is rooted in a deep mutual dependency of the people, and in the crises that occur in these dependent relationships. A Danish psychiatrist remarked to me once that Danes can be divided into two groups: those of one group are on the lookout for someone in the other group to take care of them. Motherly care is intensive and prolonged, often at the cost of the child's independence. This leads to passive behavior, even in adults, a passivity that is often mocked in Danish cartoons. In the relationship between the sexes, the ideas of friendship and of being cared for and protected play an important role. Marital crises often stem from disappointment in the expectations of being cared for and protected, because each partner expects to be mothered as a child by the other. As for dreaming and waking fantasies, people frequently report imagining a reunion with a spouse after death. Although the population is not deeply attached to the church, and most of the persons investigated described themselves as "not religious," the religious concepts relating to a life after death and reunion with dead relatives are believed in by most of the people. Andersen's fairy tales, in which death often occurs as the crowning event, were created out of this emotional climate. The Little Match Girl goes to join her dead grandmother in heaven. In death, the Steadfast Tin Soldier is united with the paper ballerina.

How, then, does Danish public opinion view suicide? In a way that is similar to the attitude prevalent in America. One does not have to be ashamed of having attempted suicide. One finds understanding, not rejection. The Christian condemnation of suicide is scarcely detected. Sympathy is felt, for suicidal crises arise when a person is threatened with abandonment, or is actually abandoned through the death of a partner, by divorce, or by separation. Aggressive tensions are not lived out; instead, the tendency is rather to kill by silence; and to ignore the other so that he feels abandoned.

How is suicide judged in Sweden? In general, the judgment is harsher than in Denmark. Suicide is regarded as an act of cowardice and failure, and is therefore a disgrace. It is not viewed, however, as disobedience to a god-given commandment. An unsatisfactory achievement, or lack of success in life or in marriage have been found to be typical motives for suicide; for this reason, both the patient and his relatives are more likely to disguise a suicide or suicide attempt in Sweden than in Denmark.

On the other hand, longing for and fantasizing about a reunion with relatives after death, which is typical of Danes, is significantly less common among the Swedes.

Swedish suicides are connected with an early dissolution of the mother-child relationship, with the emphasis on independence, achievement, and self-control. In other words, the same basic Swedish characteristics that have secured Sweden world wide respect in science, literature, and economics, have also raised the suicide rate to its present high level.

The Norwegian character differs from the Danish and Swedish primarily in its expansive behavior. Norwegian children are not brought up with the idea that they have to be loving and well behaved, as the Danish children are; nor must they be self-controlled and correct, like the Swedish. Norwegian children are expected to love one another, and to defend themselves and fight recklessly among themselves. The Norwegian also differs from his neighbours in his attitudes toward achievement and success, which are rather unrealistic and fantastic. A patient will wish to win a big lottery, or dream of fantastic good fortune that comes to him as if he were a hero of some fairy tale from his childhood.

Children are the chief content of a Norwegian mother's life, but she encourages their early independence.

In *Peer Gynt,* Ibsen created a figure who shows many aspects of the basic Norwegian character. From childhood to death, Peer lives more in a fantastic world than in a real fulfillment. His mother nurtures his dreaming and planning, and accompanies the wild boy on his fantasized sledge journey through a lengendary land.

An affirmation of life and a sense of self-assurance are largely dependent on childhood and maternal attitudes. The Norwegian's emotional equilibrium seems to be encouraged by the kind of mother-child relationships in that society. They are just as intimate and lasting as in Denmark, but do not lead to dependency and passivity. On the contrary, they set the child free, by encouraging early independence. For centuries, Norwegians have been sailors and adventurers, and until recently more people emigrated from Norway than from the other Scandinavian countries. Indeed, emigration has been suggested as an explanation for Norway's low suicide rate. The theory is, that high emigration was a way for the maladjusted, discontented, psychically-labile people to escape, leaving the healthy, stable, well adjusted at home. It can be shown, however, that rates of emigration and incidences of suicide are not reciprocally related. Further investigation of the suicide rates of immigrants from the Scandinavian countries to America have shown that even here the Danes have a suicide rate that is twice as high as that of the Norwegians.

The differences among the three countries can be summarized as follows:

While the mother-child relationship in Norway is similar to that in Denmark, there are, nevertheless, significant differences. In Norway, as in Sweden, the child's independence is highly valued, and for this reason, his full development is seldom checked. The mother's feeling is primarily directed toward her child, but this is counterbalanced by her wish to have a maximally independent child. In comparison with the Swedish child, the Norwegian child does not view this push toward an early independence as a lack of love, as is often the case in Sweden; as a result, the Norwegian is not as dependent on the permanence of his ties to his mother, so he bears his loss better than a Dane.

In contrast to both its neighbouring countries, Norwegian upbringing is distinguished by a greater tolerance toward the child's need to experience all of his feelings. He is allowed to feel tender and affectionate behavior and to defend himself—that is, he may fight and love without a bad conscience, speak about his loves and hates and tensions, and live them out without guilt. Finally, the Norwegian does not live under the imperative to achieve and to succeed as does the Swede. Seldom does a Norwegian kill himself as a punishment for his failure in life or for a failure to live up to expectations.

The second striking piece of evidence for the constancy of partial suicide as preceding practically all total suicides comes from Poldinger's significant but unsuccessful attempt to evaluate the risk of suicide. On the basis of an investigation of 1157 patients in the University Clinic in Basel, Poldinger worked out a "Table of Risks" in which different factors which encourage a suicide attempt are listed in order of increasing importance. At first, Poldinger believed he had found an instrument that would enable any medical practitioner to assess the risk of suicide of any patient. His Table of Risks runs like this:

1. Male
2. Female
3. Under 45 years of age
4. Over 45 years of age
5. Single
6. Married
7. Widowed
8. Divorced or separated
9. Without ties to a religious denomination
10. Family difficulties
11. Problems in love, marriage, or sex
12. Professional difficulties
13. Financial Difficulties
14. Illness or delusions of illness; chronic pain
15. Biological crises—puberty, climacterium, pregnancy
16. Loneliness—sick of life
17. Isolation, imprisonment
18. Earlier suicide attempts
19. Threats of suicide; thoughts of suicide
20. Fantasies and dreams of death and dying
21. Suicide in the family or surroundings
22. Anxiety
23. Inability to express aggression
24. Obstinate sleeplessness
25. Alchohol abuse
26. Drug abuse
27. Reactive depression (psychogenic)
28. Nonreactive depression (endogenous)

29. Psychopathic personality
30. Neurotic character disturbance
31. Chronic alchoholism
32. Drug addiction
33. Schizophrenia

Poldinger thought it possible to calculate the risk of suicide by adding the values for the factors present for each patient. If they add up to over 100, the risk of suicide is high, and hospitalization is recommended.

If the values are between 50 and 100, the risk of suicide is low, but nevertheless significant. Hospitalization or treatment on an out-patient basis is advisable, depending on the conditions of his surrounding, and the possibility of relatives taking care of him. If the values are below 50, the risk of suicide is minimal.

Poldinger himself, however, adds that this list is only meaningful when it is seen in the broader context of a thorough clinical exploration and extended diagnosis.

In 1970 and 1971, Padrutt and Kind, in the Psychiatric Polyklinik of the University of Zurich, investigated 237 patients who had made serious attempts to commit suicide. They were able to show convincingly that Poldinger's Table of Risks was practically useless and sometimes even deceptive. In the course of their investigations, they discovered—and it is this discovery that is significant here—that "The evaluation of the risk of suicide is decisively dependent on whether the formal clinical exploration situation becomes transformed into a human encounter between fellow human beings...." The apparent paradox is observed, that the more we know about a patient, the more he shows us of his feeling and motivation, the more we become, in Sullivan's sense, an involved and participating observer, and not merely an aloof, distant investigator of events. Thereby, the risk of suicide is substantially changed and reduced in the course of the interview itself, because every exploratory interview is already a therapeutic intervention, that breaks through the patient's isolation from his fellow human beings.

Scharfetter, too, notes that a fleeing *from* death (mere survival) and a fleeing *into* death (suicide) are not at all contrasting and mutually exclusive modes of human behavior, as at first glance they might seem to be. Rather, mere survival is an existential partial suicide, and almost always a necessary precursor of total suicide. Scharfetter distinguishes between the number of suicides and the suicide rates, and concludes that suicide is approximately the tenth most frequent cause of death.

The figures quoted in the literature for the ratio of suicide to suicide attempts vary from 1:3 to 1:10. According to the W.H.O. (1962), suicide rates in different countries range between the extremes of 0.1 (Arabian states) and 35.9 (West Berlin). In the European countries, England, and Scandinavia, the rate lies between 10 and 25. For years the suicide rates have steadily risen. This is dependent, among other factors, on better methods of registration, and an excessive proportion of old people. Suicide occurs more frequently at certain times of the year. In this way it resembles the affect psychoses which also have a peak incidence in spring and autumn. The ratio of suicides in men and women is 2-4:1; for attempted suicide, it is 1:2. This means that women attempt suicide about twice as often as men, but that men's attempts are more frequently successful. Before 15 years of age, suicide is very rare. The average age for suicides is 55-60, for suicide attempts between 30 and 55. People in the periods of biological crises, (puberty, youth, the climacterium, and beginning senility), are more inclined to commit suicide.

Solitary people have the highest suicide rate. Married people, especially those with children, have the lowest. Unmarried people commit suicide about twice as frequently as married people, while divorcees and widowed people about 4-5 times more often.

There is a tendency for an increased incidence of suicide in the highest and lowest classes, while in the middle classes there are peak incidences in certain professions—for instance, medical practitioners. The rate is extremely high among students (every third death). The suicide rate in cities is substantially higher than in the country. Immigrants commit suicide more frequently than the indigenous in the United States. It must be added, though, that the rate among immigrants is similar to that for their land of origin. The significance of religion in an act of suicide or attempted suicide is much disputed. Some Catholic lands (Spain and Italy) have low rates, while others (Austria and France) have high or medium rates. Among the Islamic peoples, suicide is rare, Certainly, religion is only one of numerous factors influencing suicide. An intense sense of security arising from religion, as well as a sense of belonging in religious minority groups, provides a certain protection against suicide.

Gruhle describes a geography of suicide, and attributes the differences in suicide rates in different parts of a country to differences in the character of the people. However, various other factors that might influence the incidence of suicide must be evaluated before hypotheses about the character of the people can be formed. In Great Britain for instance, the Scots have always had a lower suicide rate than the English; but the method of registering deaths in Scotland favors suppression of suicide as a stated cause of death. In Europe, toxic agents, especially sedatives, are by far the commonest agents used by suicides. In the United States, guns are the most common agents.

Any investigation of suicide has to distinguish between cause and motive, and has to account for a predisposition to an act of suicide. In respect to cause, the connection between suicide and the endogenous psychoses is important. It is, however, difficult to say how many suicides suffered from an endogenous psychosis. The figures quoted in the literature range from 6-66 per cent. As an approximate estimate, between one-third and one-half of suicides can be traced back to an endogenous psychosis. The proportion of depressive psychoses is higher than that of schizophrenia. For attempted suicide, the proportion of endogenous psychoses is clearly smaller; according to the literature, between 10-15 per cent. This means that acts of suicide by psychotic patients more frequently have a fatal outcome than those by nonpsychotic patients. The incidence of suicide among schizophrenics is mostly underestimated. About 19-22 per cent of schizophrenics have suicidal tendencies according to Mayer-Gross. In a 1967 review of the literature, Osmond and Hofer note that 1.8 per cent of schizophrenics commit suicide within eight years of presentation; according to Poldinger, 4 per cent commit suicide after ten years. Figures for the suicide rate among patients suffering from the different affect psychoses vary, depending on authors and periods of observation, from 3-15 per cent. Patients are most liable to commit suicide at the onset of a psychotic phase, and during the period just after discharge from a clinic.

When all psychic disturbances—neuroses, psychopathic attitudes, alchoholism, and organic brain syndromes—are included, some authors concluded that at least 94 per cent of suicide victims are in some way psychically disturbed, and at least 4 per cent are physically ill. Sainsbury noted that people with suicidal tendencies who suffer from affect psychoses have a high risk of repeated acts of suicide, and a fatal outcome; and that psychoneurotic patients with repeated suicide attempts often survive. The demographic characteristics of this second group are different from those of patients who commit suicide successfully, the proportion of women, young people, and married people being higher. Nonpsychotic people who suicide show a substantially higher incidence of stress factors in their momentary life situation.

There is no possible psychic trauma, fear, or crisis that cannot lead to an act of suicide, but any investigator must beware of a tendency to rationalize motivations. Usually a suicide is being investigated by a healthy person who attempts to make sense of it, according to his own perceptions, without the necessary insight into the emotional and developmental state of the dead person, so that the psychic state of affairs at the time of the act is viewed too rationally.

As far as the predisposition to suicide is concerned, isolation from other human beings plays an important role. Isolation means the loss of a meaningful fulfillment of human existence, which depends largely on whether a human being has a fellow human being for whom he can care, and who cares for him. Difficulties in childhood and broken homes are often cited as predisposing to a later suicide; however, it has not been clearly shown that those who suicide come more frequently from broken homes than not. Further, the broken-home situation is certainly nonspecific, and can only play a role in combination with other factors.

It has been pointed out, and with good reason, that total suicide, a fleeing from life into death, and the fleeing from death into a state of mere insensible survival, a state in which the human being loses that fundamental possibility of dying, are in no way opposites. This latter fleeing from death is already a partial suicide, such as is always present as the precursor of a total suicide.

Furthermore, what is valid for the single human being also has significance for humanity as a whole. That is to say, the technological spirit that now has almost absolute dominion over the whole planet drives human beings into the kind of relationship that is based on the ever-increasing production of measurable goods. All human beings are increasingly caught up in this constricting view of the world, and human existence is being increasingly reduced to an ever narrower realm. Such a reduction of human possibilities is, in Ringle's sense, nothing more than a presuicidal syndrome for humanity as a whole. Those with insight have already recognized presuicidal signs in the material destruction wrought on our environment. If we should ever allow this technology to establish total and absolute control over human beings, then the complete suicide of the nature of being-human—indeed the total suicide of humanity—would be certain.

REFERENCES

1. Angst, J. *Zur Aetiologie und Nosologie endogener depressiver Psychosen.* New York: Springer, 1966.

2. Boss, M. *Grundriss der Medizin.* Bern-Stuttgart: Hans Huber, 1972.

3. Hendin, H. *Suicide and Scandinavia.* New York: Grune & Stratton, 1964.

4. Haffter, C., Waage,G. and Zumpe, L. *Selbstmordversuche bei Kindern und Jungendlichen.* Basel: S. Karger, 1966.

5. Hofmann, T. *Katamnesen nach Suizidversuch.* Bern: Hallwag, 1971.

6. Kind, H. *"Früherkennung des Suizidrisikos und prophylaktishe Massnahmen," Praxis der Psychotherapie.* XVI (1971), 175-84.

7. Mayer-Gross, W., and Slater, E. Roth: *Clinical Psychiatry.* London: Cassell, 1960.

8. Osmond, H., and Hoffer, A. *"Schizophrenia and Suicide," J. Schizophr.* I (1967), 54-65.

9. Perris, C. *A Study of Bipolar (Manic-Depressive) and Unipolar Recurrent Depressive Psychosis.* Copenhagen: Munksgaart, 1966.

10. Pradrutt, H.P. *Die Abschatzung der Suizidalität.* Bern: Hallwag, 1970.

11. Poldinger, W. *Die Abschatzung der Suicidalitat.* Bern-Stuttgart: Huber, 1968.

12. Ringel, E. *Selbstmordverhütung.* Bern-Stuttgart-Wien: Huber, 1969.

13. Sainsbury, P. "Suicide and Depression," in, A. Cappan, A. Walk (eds), "Recent developments in affective disorders," *Brit J. Psychiat,* Spec. Publ. No. 2, 1-13.

14. Stengel, E., and Cook, N.G. *Attempted Suicide.* London: Chapman & Hall, 1958.

15. Stengel, E. "Selbstmord und Selbstmordversuch," *Psychiatrie der Gegenwart,* III (1966).

II
Suicide—A Psychosocial Phenomenon

HERBERT H. KRAUSS

There is but one truly serious philosophical problem, and that is suicide. Judging whether life is or is not worth living amounts to answering the fundamental question of philosophy. All the rest—whether or not the world has three dimensions, whether the mind has nine or twelve categories—comes afterwards—Camus

WHAT IS THE NATURE OF SUICIDE? IF ONE SEEKS THE ANSWER BY studying case histories drawn from a variety of cultures, a number of paradoxes arise. Suicide appears to be at once the most private of acts and the most public. The most egocentric and the most altruistic of acts. The most compassionate and the most vengeful of acts. The most meaningful and the most meaningless of acts. Suicide marks the boldest renunciation of life and life's boldest reaffirmation. Suicide appears to spring from the simplest, most primitive of emotions and takes place within a field of overwhelming complexity.

Consider these facts and stories.

Apache parents loved their children deeply. When an Apache prayed, his first words were entreaties for the continued good health and well-being of his children. The loss of a child was considered disastrous. The story is told of a widow living at Bylas. She had only one son. The young man was unmarried and lived with her. One

winter he was taken sick. The woman did everything she could think of to save him. Shamans worked over him, but to no avail. Finally, he died. They buried him the next day. A few days later the woman told neighbors she was going over the river to get something. The neighbors noticed that she had not returned by the following day. They set out in search of her and found her across the river hanging from a tree. She was so despondent she had hung herself.

Suicide was uncommon among the Kababish, an Arab tribe living in the Sudan. But it does occur: "A man of *el-Hammadab khasm beyt* went a little ways from the ferik and opened his belly with a knife. He did this because his father would not consent to his marriage with the girl upon whom his heart was set. His death came as a surprise, for although he had told his father several times that he would take his life if his father did not yield, it was not expected that he could carry out his threat. After his death, public opinion went strongly against his father" (51).

Life was hard for the Chukchee of Siberia. Anyone who believed himself to be seriously injured or ill, or too old to look after himself, anyone who doubted his ability to cope on the tundra, might choose suicide:

"One summer, while I was at Marlinsky Post, a large skin boat from the Telga 'p tundra arrived for trading purposes. One of the newcomers, after a visit to the Russian barracks, felt a sudden pain in his stomach. During the night the pain became acute, the sufferer asked to be killed, and his fellow travellers complied with his request" (4).

The Cheyenne were often at war, and such warfare often set the scene for suicidal behavior:

"Touching. . .is the story of the old blind man, Spit, who at the Wagon-Box Fight with the United States Army said he was always looking for just such a chance to die, for he was tired of only half seeing his way; where were the soldiers? Young ones took his hand, lined his face toward the firing enemy. Serene, he walked toward his death, until a bullet brought it to him" (28).

Suicide seems a universal phenomenon and a complex phenomenon. Some cultures forbid suicide, some demand it and ritualize it, as in suttee in India. Some individuals yield to the rules and prohibitions of their cultures, some resist them. Some commit suicide in reaction to hardship, others despite success.

The aim of theory is to reduce the paradoxical and complex nature of a problem into simple principle. To accomplish this, two major theoretical approaches to the understanding of suicide exist, each developed apart from and independent of the other. One bears the unmistakable imprint of Sigmund Freud, the other, the imprint of Emile Durkheim. Following Freud, psychoanalytically-oriented theorists have sought the key to the mystery of suicide within the individual. Following Durkheim, sociologists have attempted to relate the incidence of suicide to the operating characteristics of society. Unfortunately, for almost seventy years and for artificial reasons, little effort has been directed toward producing a synthesis of these parallel efforts. No unified theory of suicidal behavior exists.

In the sections that follow, Freud's intrapsychic and Durkheim's sociological theories are reviewed and compared. More recent theories (Naroll, Dollard, and others) deriving from their groundwork are discussed. Finally, an attempt is made to show how social and psychological theories can be unified to give a picture of suicide as an act of a psychologically vulnerable individual responding to particular types of characteristic, socially-programmed stresses in his society. The self-destructive person, then, stands at the crosshairs of his character and his culture.

Freud and Suicide

Freud produced no monograph on suicide. Nowhere does he present a complete statement of his thoughts on the matter. In fact, two different interpretations of suicide have been linked to his name. Each interpretation is characterized by Freud's intense need to rationalize his own life's experience, and is marked by his preoccupation with what Erikson (12) has termed the "inward," "backward," and "downward" focus upon man's inner world, the ontogenesis of mind, and the instinctual basis of behavior.

The earliest of Freud's theoretical contributions to the understanding of suicide is foreshadowed in a letter to Martha Bernays, his intended wife. The letter concerns the death of a colleague (16):

...on the thirteenth he hanged himself. What drove him to it?

As an explanation, the world is ready to hurl the most ghastly accusations at the unfortunate widow. I don't believe in them. I believe that the realization of an enormous failure, the rage caused by rejected passion, the fury at having sacrificed his whole scientific career, his entire fortune, for a domestic disaster, perhaps also the annoyance at having been done out of the promised dowry, as well as the inability to face the world and confess it all—I believe that all of this, following a number of scenes which opened his eyes to his situation, may have brought this madly vain man (who in any case was given to serious emotional upheavals) to the brink of despair. He died from the sum total of his qualities, his pathological self-love coupled with the claims he made for the higher things in life.

Freud saw the death of his colleague as a result of the cumulative frustrations of a life style that demanded too much of him. He died because he turned his rage at those frustrations against himself. He died because of his pride, his vanity, and his narcissism.

In "Mourning and Melancholia," Freud compared the normal reaction to the loss of a loved one or a cherished idea or goal, and pathological melancholia. According to Freud, mourning and melancholia differ in that, in mourning, the world is seen by the aggrieved as poor and empty, while in melancholia it is the ego itself which is depleted. Menninger (42) describes the two conditions as follows:

> The normal person reacts [to loss] for a time with grief, that is, he feels as if something beautiful and desirable in the world has been taken away from him, leaving life poorer for its loss. Time heals such wounds...everyday the pain and bereavement grows less. But in melancholia the loss of a loved one, not necessarily by death, in fact more often by jilting, results in a different sort of reaction. There is the same brooding sadness but with a different content which grows greater instead of less. It is not the world that seems poor and empty, it is something inside of the individual himself. He complains that he feels worthless, miserable, and wretched. He often says he ought not to be allowed to live and asks himself to be taken to prison or to the gallows. It is clear that he hates himself.

Emily Dickinson (8) distilled the essence of melancholia in her poem, *I felt a Funeral in My Brain.*

I felt a Funeral, in my brain,
And mourners to and fro
Kept treading—treading till it seemed
That sense was breaking through—

And when they all were seated,
A service, like a drum—
Kept beating—beating till I thought
My mind was going numb—

And then I heard them lift a box
And creak across my soul
With those same boots of lead, again
Then space—began to tell,

As all the heavens were a bell,
And being, but an ear,
And I, and silence, some strange race
Wrecked, solitary, here—

And then a plank in reason broke,
And I dropped down, and down—
And hit a world, at every plunge,
And finished knowing—then—

Having contrasted melancholia to the normal reaction to loss, Freud (15) sketched the process underlying melancholia as follows:

First there existed an object choice, the libido had attached itself to a certain person; then, owing to a real injury or disappointment concerned with the loved person, this object-relationship was undermined. The result was not the normal one of withdrawal of the libido from this object and transference of it to a new one, but something different for which various conditions seem to be necessary. The object-cathexis proved to have little power of resistance, and was abandoned; but the free libido was withdrawn into the ego and not directed to another object. It did not find application there, however, in any one of several possible ways, but served simply to establish an *identification* of the ego with the abandoned object. Thus the shadow of the object fell upon the ego, so that the latter could henceforth be criticized by a special mental faculty like an object, like the forsaken object. In this way the loss of the object became transformed into a loss in the ego, and the conflict between the ego and the loved person transformed into a cleavage between the criticizing faculty of the ego and the ego as altered by the identification.

Such a situation, Freud argues, could occur only if the individual has had an extremely intense but fragile attachment to the lost object. Freud identifies this condition as symptomatic of a particular configuration of personality development, one in which "narcissistic" trends predominate.

Freud proposed that in normal development a part of the ego becomes, in effect, the ultimate reality, capable of fulfilling every need—the outlook of the narcissists. Another part, however, recognizes the existence of other, real individuals (such as the mother) to whom one could look for aid in gratifying instinctual desires—the anaclitic mode of development. Thus, in normal development a reasonable balance exists between self-esteem and an appreciation of objective reality. Unfortunately, and for a variety of reasons, such as a rejecting or over-indulgent mother, a genetic predisposition, or some other noxious configuration, the ego may adopt the narcissistic manner of relating to reality instead of a balanced parallel development.

In the Freudian schema, narcissistic attachments to external objects are characterized by their fragility. These attachments are likely to be severed when they no longer serve the narcissists' exacting demands for gratification. Since the narcissist is not omnipotent, though he may think he is, he is continually threatened by frustration. Hesse (27) put it this way:

> What is peculiar to the suicide is that his ego, rightly or wrongly, is felt to be an extremely dangerous, dubious, and doomed germ of nature; that he is always in his own eyes exposed to an extraordinary risk, as though he stood with the slightest foothold on the peak of a crag whence a slight push from without or an instant's weakness from within suffices to precipitate him into the void.

Because the narcissist feels that no one exists but himself, the anger that the narcissist experiences as a consequence of frustration eventually must be turned against himself. When he experiences frustration at the hands of an object with which he narcissistically identifies, Freud suggests (17): "The melancholic's erotic cathexis of his object thus undergoes a twofold fate: a part of it regresses to identification, but the other part, under the influence of the conflict of ambivalence, is reduced to the stage of sadism...."

If the animosity and hatred generated against the portion of the ego with which the object is identified is great enough, the ego acts to destroy that identification, and in so doing destroys itself.

Thus, Freud's earliest view of suicide may be summarized by the phrase, "narcissism-frustrated." Suicide results, according to this model, when an individual, enraged by his having been denied a cherished goal or relationship, destroys the representation of that goal or object within himself and thereby destroys himself.

The death-instinct hypothesis. The postulation of a death instinct was Freud's second contribution to a theory of suicide. Foreshadowed in earlier works, the death instinct theory finally achieved shape in *Beyond the Pleasure Principle*, a work born in the shadow of the First World War and two deaths—his daughter Sophie's, and his friend and patient, Anton Von Freund's. In this work, Freud drew upon his own preoccupation with death, his clinical experience with post-traumatic dreams, patients who compulsively repeated painful events, and what he termed "fate neuroses," in which an individual seems to be led from one tragedy to another.

To Freud, the death instinct, *thanatos,* was as basic a force as *eros,* the life drive. The aim of the death instinct is to return the organism to a state of quiescence, to promote entropy. For life to be maintained, *eros* must predominate; but as one grows older, *thanatos* begins to gain ascendancy until death occurs. The relationship of *eros* and *thanatos* is more complex than I have indicated, as may be seen from Freud's essay, *The Economic Problems of Masochism* (20):

> The original quantity of internalized death instinct is identical with masochism. The individual tries to externalize this energy as aggression or sadism. Where there is a cultural suppression of the instincts, the destructive instinctual components are turned back into his superego. Now we see a helpless, masochistic ego in

relationship with a sadistic superego. The modality of the relationship is punishment. In order to provoke punishment, The masochist must do what is inexpedient, must act against his own interest, must ruin his prospects and perhaps destroy himself. Since there is always some fusion of the erotic and destructive instincts, there is always an obvious erotic component in masochism, so that even the subject's destruction of himself cannot take place without libidinal satisfaction.

The relationship between *thanatos* and suicide was summed up by Meerloo (41); "Suicide represents the precocious victory of the inner drive toward death."

Few psychoanalysts have accepted Freud's construct of the death instinct (32), and not many more have accepted it even in a modified form. Menninger (42, 43), Meerloo (41), and Futterman (21) are among the exceptions. In spite of their work, however, the concept of a death instinct, aside from some theoretical and meta-psychological interest, has had little impact on the scientific investigation of suicide. The notable exceptions are in the fields of accident research, where the death instinct has been invoked to understand the relationship between acidental injuries and suicide.

However utilitarian the death instinct theory may appear, the inherent contradiction between an instinct for death and the therapist's commitment to life has prevented most therapists from incorporating *thanatos* into their explanation of suicidal behavior.

DURKHEIM

Many parallels may be drawn between Freud and Durkheim. They were, to begin with, contemporaries. They were also both secularized Jews who attempted, through rational analysis, to understand and give meaning to the turmoil of their times. They were moralists and reformers who wished to reduce man's suffering. Both labored to create an institutional framework for viewing and comprehending human behavior—in Freud's case, psychoanalysis, in Durkheim's case, the French school of sociology. While Freud looked at man in terms of biology and evolutionary theory, Durkheim looked at man in terms of society, the supra-organic whole which he believed stamped out and engineered man's existence.

Durkheim's biographer, La Capra, saw the impetus behind Durkheim's work as his need to discover a solution for the problems posed to man by modern industrial society (35).

> For him [Durkheim] the problem of a just social order in modern society presented itself very much in the light of rational specification of the principles of the French Revolution in terms which would enable man to humanize and absorb the industrial revolution. The moral mission of sociology itself was to provide, through an analytic and comparative study of institutions and values, orientations in reaching this goal.

The forces which operated to focus Durkheim's interest in that task, and caused him to seek the heart of the matter in the nature and structure of society will, of course, never be known in their entirety. Perhaps, as La Capra suggests, the disintegration of the Jewish ghettoes of eastern France influenced the direction of Durkheim's thought. Perhaps the loss of *patrie,* attendant upon the Franco-Prussian War, contributed to the process. Perhaps the philosophical renaissance occurring at the Ecole Normale during his attendance there, or his work with Wundt in ethics, or the "socialists of the chair" with whom he studied in Germany influenced his direction. Nonetheless, he did, indeed, turn outward, and in so doing rediscovered and elaborated upon Comte's idea that societies maintain their coherence only through common belief (1).

In his classic, *Suicide,* Durkheim used this discovery to suggest that self-inflicted death might be better viewed as a consequence of social structure than as a purely capricious and individual act (10):

But it seems hardly possible to us that there will not emerge, on the contrary, from every page of this book, so to speak, the impression that the individual is dominated by a moral reality greater than himself: namely, collective reality. When each people is seen to have its own suicide-rate, more constant than that of general mortality; that its growth is in accordance with coefficient of acceleration characteristic of each society; when it appears that the variations through which it passes at different times of the day, month, year, merely reflect the rhythm of social life; and that marriage, divorce, the family, religious society, the army, etc. affect it in accordance with definite laws, some of which may even be numerically expressed—these states and institutions will no longer be regarded simply as characterless, ineffective ideological arrangements. Rather they will be felt to be real, living, active forces which, because of the way they determine the individual, prove their independence of him, which if the individual enters as an element in the combination whence these forces ensue, at least control him once they are formed. Thus it would appear more clearly why sociology can and must be objective, since it deals with realities as definite and substantial as those of the psychologist or the biologist.

The raw data for Durkheim's analysis were the rates of suicide for various countries, ethnic and religious groups, marital statuses, and psychopathological conditions. Seasonal, monthly, and daily fluctuations in the rate of suicide were also analyzed. His conslusion was that neither heredity, seasonal variation, insanity, nor alchoholism could be considered the direct cause of suicide. The rate of suicide was, therefore, a function of the way in which a society was constructed.

From his intutitive factor analysis of suicide rates, Durkheim identified two dimensions of societal structure relevant to suicide: the first, a social integration factor; the second, a vulnerability to deregulation factor. *Egoistic* and *altruistic suicide* occur at the poles of the first dimension, and *anomic* and *fatalistic suicide* at the poles of the second.

Egoistic suicide. Durkheim found that Jews committed suicide less often than did Catholics, and Catholics committed suicide less often than did Protestants. Further, the rate of suicide appeared to vary with the degree to which the individual was embedded within a stable domestic life (divorcees were more prone to suicide) and within a stable political life (countries with stable governments had lower rates of suicide). From these observations, Durkheim concluded that "suicide varies inversely with the degree of integration of social groups of which the individual forms a part".

This relationship between suicide and social integration existed, Durkheim argued, because man's *raison d'etre* was intimately linked to "social interest." Societies lacking in integration deprived man of his meaning in life. In addition, he felt that the form of individualism most frequently associated with loosely integrated societies "freed" man from the social proscription (it is evil to kill yourself) against taking his own life. Thus, in loosely integrated societies, not only did the efforts of individuals to give meaning to their lives often prove inadequate, but in a figurative sense, they were given permission to take their own lives. Durkheim termed these suicides *egoistic.*

Altruistic suicide. The opposite of egoistic suicide is *altruistic* suicide. Altruistic suicide is the result of societies that are well integrated. A member of such a society is prone to kill himself in pursuit of suprapersonal goals. The Japanese custom of *hari-kiri* and the Hindu practice of *suttee* are examples of altruistic suicide. The origin of *suttee* is described by Zimmer (56):

> *Sati* was the name assumed by the universal Goddess when she became incarnate as the daughter of the old divinity Daksa in order to become the perfect wife of Siva. And sati, furthermore, is the Sanskrit original form of the word that in English now

is "suttee," denoting the self-immolation of the Hindu widow in her husband's funeral pyre—an act of consummating the perfect identification of the individual with her role, as a living image of romantic Hindu ideal of her spouse. Her lord, her enlivening principle, having passed away, her remaining body can only be *a-sat, non-sat:* "unreal, non-existent, false, untrue, improper; not answering its purpose; bad, wicked, evil, vile."

Anomic suicide. Durkheim considered *anomie* to be a state of de-regulation—not "meaninglessness," as the term is currently employed by many investigators, for instance, Powell. Anomie occurs when the normal controls that a society exerts upon the individual in general, and his passions in particular, are lessened. Divorce, for example, is often the occasion for anomie.

Now divorce implies a weakening of matrimonial regulations. Where it exists, and especially where law and custom permit its excessive practice, marriage is nothing but a weakened simulacrum of itself; it is an inferior form of marriage. It cannot produce its useful effects to the same degree. Its restraint upon desire is weakened; since it is more easily disturbed and superceded, it controls passion less and passion tends to rebel. It consents less readily to its assigned limit. The moral calmness and tranquility which were the husband's strength are less; they are replaced to some extent by an uneasiness which keeps a man from being satisfied with what he has. Besides, he is the less inclined to become attached to his present state of his enjoyment if it is not completely sure, the future is less certain. One cannot be strongly restrained by a chain which may be broken on one side or the other at any moment. One cannot help looking beyond one's own position when the ground underfoot does not feel secure. Hence, in the countries where marriage is strongly tempered by divorce, the immunity of the married man is inevitably less. As he resembles the unmarried under this regime, he inevitably loses some of his advantages. Consequently, the total number of suicides rises.

Fatalistic suicide. The last case in Durkheim's typology of suicide is *fatalistic* suicide. Fatalistic suicide is a consequence of excessively oppressive regulation; it is the suicide "...of persons with futures pitilessly blocked and passions violently choked by oppressive discipline....Do not the suicides of slaves, said to be frequent under certain conditions...belong to this type, or all suicides attributable to excessive physical or moral despotism?"

Lewin (37) used somewhat different terms to describe such suicide, but the similarity of his formulation to that of Durkheim's is clear. "If the barrier is very firm, there is no way out for the child. Under these conditions and with sufficiently strong tension in the total field, there may develop tendencies toward suicide. Suicide then appears as the last remaining possibility of going-out-of-the-field."

Synthesizing the Individual and Social Theories of Suicide. Both Durkheim and Freud were major theoretical contributors to the literature of suicide; each offered a well-differentiated view of suicide; each, however, stressed different components of the suicidal act. Their disagreement is an old one. Simmel (52) put it this way:

> There is an old conflict over the nature of society. One side mystically exaggerates its significance, contending that only through society is human life endowed with reality. The other regards it as a mere abstract concept by means of which the observer draws the realities, which are individual human beings, into a whole, as one calls trees and books, houses and meadows, "landscape." However one decides this conflict, he must allow society to be a reality in a double sense. On the one hand are the individuals in their directly perceptible existence, the bearers of the processes of association, who are united by these processes into the higher unity which one calls "society"; on the

other hand, the interests which, living in the individual, motivate such union: economic and ideal interests, warlike and erotic, religious and charitable. To satisfy such urges and to attain such purposes arise the innumerable forms of social life....

One way of choosing between Freud's psychological view and Durkheim's sociological conceptualization of suicide is to recognize that both views are complementary and not antagonistic. In fact, the necessity of synthesizing the two theoretical postures for the construction of a comprehensive theory of suicide has long been recognized. Simpson (53) suggested, for example, "that interrelating psychoanalytic discoveries on the motives for suicide with the conditions under which suicide occurs, offers the most fruitful method of advancing our knowledge of the phenomenon." More than a few theorists have attempted such a synthesis. The most successful have simplified Freud's position along the lines suggested by Dollard *et al* (9), emphasizing the importance of frustration in leading to self-directed aggression and therefore to suicide.

DOLLARD

In their reformulation of Freud's frustration-narcissism hypothesis, a view which has seen little modification over time, Dollard and his co-workers employed the language of learning theory, not psychoanalysis. They posited that aggressive behavior is the natural result of frustration, frustration being defined as "an interference with the occurence of an instigated goal-response at its proper time in the behavior sequence." The degree of frustration generated varies with (1) the strength of the goal-directed behavior; (2) the extent to which that behavior is the subject of interference; and (3) the number of response sequences that are frustrated.

The natural, unimpeded reaction to frustration is aggressive activity directed toward the frustrating agent. An individual who has been punished for outward aggressive behavior with the loss, or injury, of one he loves, with the threat of failure, or with a noxious stimulus, may inhibit this direct response and delay or disguise or divert it.

For Dollard, suicide occurs when frustration-produced aggression is turned inward, and the self, for whatever reason, becomes the target of its own rage.

NAROLL'S THWARTING-DISORIENTATION HYPOTHESIS

Can Durkheim's sociological approach to suicide be combined with a frustration-aggression theory?

Naroll (45, 46) has attempted to do this with his *thwarting-disorientation* theory of suicide. In this work, Naroll tried to give social and interpersonal definition to the type of frustration which is likely to precipitate suicide. He then tried to identify some socially accepted and culturally normative contexts which might generate this interpersonal frustration.

"We propose to consider some sociological contexts. Let us call them contexts of *thwarting disorientation.* The contexts involve two major components: (1) they are siutations in which a person's social ties are broken, weakened, or threatened, and (2) they are also situations involving the thwarting of the disoriented person by some person" (46).

He identified seven such contexts; (1) wifebeating; (2) marriage restriction; (3) men's divorce freedom; (4) witchcraft accusation; (5) drunken brawling; (6) defiant homicide; and (7) frequent warfare, acknowledging that there were undoubtedly others. In these situations, it would be likely that person's social ties would be threatened by an identifiable other person. Witchcraft accusation, for example, produced thwarting disorientation in two ways:

First, for the point of view of a person accused of committing witchcraft: such a person is commonly subject to capital punishment and certainly would be feared and shunned by those of his associates who credit the accusation. The spouse and children of a person executed for witchcraft would suffer social disorientation from the death. Second, from the point of view of the family of a person who in fact died of disease: In societies in which witchcraft attribution is a common explanation of illness, people would often explain the natural death of a loved family member as the effect of witchcraft by some suspected witch. They would then perceive their situation as a thwarting disorientation context, even though a person believing, for example, in the germ theory of infectious disease would not.

Next, he determined that in a random sample of 58 societies, mostly primitive tribes, a direct relationship existed between the presence of these traits in a society and an index of that society's rate of suicide. The greater the number of thwarting-disorientation traits present, the higher the society's rate of suicide. Support for Naroll's thwarting-disorientation hypothesis also comes from the work of Krauss (33, 34) who, following Naroll's lead, discovered from an analysis of suicide case histories that individuals most frequently commit suicide after their interpersonal ties have been threatened or ruptured. This finding has been confirmed by other investigators.

If the above line of reasoning is carried to its conclusion, Durkheim's typology of suicide may be recast in terms of Naroll's modification of Dollard's frustration-aggression hypothesis, a modification which amplifies the importance of interpersonal frustration to the suicidal act. Before doing this, an explanation as to why interpersonal frustration is central to suicidal behavior seems in order.

THE IMPORTANCE OF INTERPERSONAL FRUSTRATION

The importance of people to people can be rationalized on a number of grounds. One line of argumentation (2, 50) suggests that man's evolutionary history requires him to enter into close relationships with those of his kind, the infant-mothering being one interaction upon which later socialization depends:

"The long period of helplessness in the human infant and child—in many respects lasting about one-sixth of the total life span—requires the development of an elaborate set of help-seeking behaviors. These are paralleled in the behavioral repertoire of the dyadic partners by help-giving reciprocals. Commonly the child's actions have been called *succorant* or *dependent,* and the partners' *nurturant*" (50).

There is evidence to show that the disruption of "normal" interaction patterns, especially early in life, may lead to defective development both biologically and socially.

Still another line of reasoning stresses the importance of close interpersonal interaction to the development of the individual's sense of both "internal" and "external" reality. Lecky (36) noted that:

>...the ability to foresee and predict environmental happenings, to understand the world one lives in and thus to be able to anticipate events and prevent the necessity for sudden readjustments, is an absolute prerequisite for the maintenance of unity. The Subject must feel that he lives in a stable and intelligible environment in which he knows what to do and how to do it, and his attitude of confidence and certainty is supported by this conviction. It is therefore not the physical injury which causes the anxiety, but the breakdown of the scheme of understanding and prediction....

>The interpretations which serve as the basis of prediction, however, rest upon no other ground than individual experience. Immersed in an environment which he does not and cannot understand, the individual is forced to create a substitute world which he can understand [and] in which he puts his faith.

Social interaction is the vehicle by which our sense of social reality and selfhood develops. As Margaret Mead (40) expressed the thought, "The self is not something that exists first and then enters into relationship with others, but it is, so to speak, an eddy in the social current and so still a part of the current."

Sullivan (54) also arrived at a similar conclusion, though he came to it from a somewhat different path. "If another person matters as much to you as you do yourself, it is quite possible to talk to this person as you have never talked to anyone before. The freedom which comes from this expanding of one's world of satisfaction and security to include two people, linked together by love, permits investigation without fear of rebuff or humiliation, which greatly augments the consensual validation of all sorts of things."

Mead, and Sullivan thus agree that man's sense of meaning derives from the network and structure of the interpersonal attachments provided him by his society.

The question arises as to whether there are any particular patterns of interpersonal frustration associated with each of Durkheim's types of suicide, and the answer appears to be "Yes." Egoistic suicide, for example, is characteristic of societies low in social cohesion, societies in which man must find his own meaning. In these societies, close interpersonal relationships are few, tenuous, and tend toward the utilitarian. In such societies, each man is responsible only to himself. Hsu (29) has given us a picture of the interpersonal frustration such a society breeds:

When the individual is shorn of all permanent and reliable moorings among his fellowmen, his only security must come from personal success, personal superiority, and personal triumph. Those who are fortunate enough to achieve success, superiority, and triumph will, of course, bask in the sunshine. But success, superiority, and triumph on the part of some must of necessity be based upon the failure, inferiority, and defeat on the part of others. For the latter, and even for some of those who are in the process of struggling for success, superiority, and triumph, the resentment against and fear of failure, inferiority, and defeat must be widespread and often unbearable.

Not only are some men doomed to fail, but the weight of failure cannot be shared as in more closely knit societies. Hsu makes that very point in contrasting the culture of white Americans with that of Chinese Americans:

> Thus comparative rates of mental illness and of suicide among the two people are commensurate with other images in this picture of contrast between their two ways of life. The individual-centered white American rejoices in his success as a personal triumph, but his failure is correspondingly a harsh personal disaster. His emotionality produces an ecstatic happiness, but it likewise causes his moments of misery to be truly devastating. The higher rates of mental illness, suicide and attempted suicide among white Americans would therefore seem to be related to the individual's isolation from his fellows and the internal pressure of his unsatisfied emotions.
>
> The situation-centered Chinese-American shares life's ups and downs with his family and his friends. In triumphs his glory is toned down because he does not enjoy it alone, just as in disaster his misery is not so unbearable because it is mitigated by sharing. Not given to emotionality in the first place, he is less easily disturbed by adverse circumstances. Being more concerned about persons surrounding him, he is less easily driven to the road of desperation.

Societies in which altruistic suicide occurs, on the other hand, provide their culture-bearers with regularity, high social integration, and a sense of meaning and place. But in so doing, they are also more likely to produce a particular type of suicide, which is socially programmed, norm-maintenance type of suicide; the suicide of a person who violates a deeply held social norm. Malinowski (38) in describing the culture of the Trobriand Islanders depicts one instance of altruistic suicide.

Only much later was I able to discover the real meaning of these events: the boy had committed suicide. The truth was that he had broken the rules of exogamy, the partner in his crime being his maternal cousin, the daughter of his mother's sister. This had been known and generally disapproved of, but nothing was done until the girl's discarded lover, who had wanted to marry her and who felt personally injured, took the initiative. This rival threatened first to use black magic against the guilty youth, but this had not much effect. Then one evening he insulted the culprit in public—accusing him in the hearing of the whole community of incest and hurling at him certain expressions intolerable to a native.

For this there was only one remedy; only one means of escape remained to the unfortunate youth. Next morning he put on festive attire and ornamentation, climbed a coco-nut palm and addressed the community, speaking from among the palm leaves and bidding them farewell. He explained the reasons for his desperate deed and also launched forth a veiled accusation against the man who had driven him to his death, upon which it became the duty of his clansmen to avenge him. Then he wailed aloud, as is the custom, jumped from a palm some sixty feet high and was killed on the spot. There followed a fight within the village in which the rival was wounded; and the quarrel was repeated during the funeral.

The potential for interpersonal frustration among individuals or societies in the throes of anomie or deregulation are monumental. Old patterns of behaving become counterproductive. Old values are shattered, with the only constants being change and the need to adjust to that change. Opler (47) illustrates the effect of cultural breakdown upon the Apache and its relationship to interpersonal frustration and anomic suicide in very graphic terms:

In the context of cultural breakdown, of rising rates of alcoholism, mental illness, and demoralization, suicide of a most dramatic and violent sort has emerged for the Apache. The method of choice is to swallow inflammable liquid, retain a portion in the mouth, and apply a lighted match. This curious method among the Western Apache is not unknown in the least. Apparently, Apache sanctions against the concept of death have been among the last cultural conceptions to falter, but with cultural attrition occurring all along the way, when these last bastions fall, they do so with a thunder of violence. We find it most interesting, psychodynamically, that dead Apaches are believed to contaminate the living and that family tensions have of course increased in the present period. A related sociodynamic happening is that the young Apache—and suicides are by no means notable among the aged and infirm—are the most caught in the conflict of two cultures, have less reason for recourse to the older traditions, and are those most prone to a weak and insecure position in intergenerational differences. Suicide by oral immolation is the magically manipulative, depressed, and anxiously hostile psychodynamic answer, an explosive one, to sociodynamic events, equally destructive in their own way.

Fatalistic suicides may also be viewed as a consequence of interpersonal frustration. Nowhere is the capacity for interpersonal frustration more pronounced than in circumstances in which a man's very existence depends upon another's whims. One only has to read of the concentration camps, whether they be German, Russian, or Vietnamese to understand terror. Surprisingly, perhaps, the rate of suicide in such circumstances appears lower than one would expect (7, 47), until one considers that in such circumstances suicide may be an act of hope and a reaffirmation of individual freedom, instead of an act of despair. One hardly has to commit suicide when his captors are willing and able to end his life for him. The common thread, therefore, which underlies each of Durkheim's types of suicide and binds them together is what we call interpersonal frustration.

INTERPERSONAL FRUSTRATION THEORY OF SUICIDE

The thrust of this paper has been directed toward bolstering the plausibility of the hypothesis that the disruption, or threatened disruption, of interpersonal ties lies at the core of the self-destructive act. Because interpersonal ties are deemed crucial to the individual's sense of personal and social meaning, the disruption of those ties spells catastrophe for the individual. This is not to say that impersonal forces, the weather, economic conditions, or disease, are unimportant. They are important inasmuch as they may create a climate in which interpersonal ties are more than normally strained.

Several propositions follow from these hypotheses.

(1) It appears that certain individuals, as a consequence of their developmental history, are more vulnerable to interpersonal frustration than others. The most vulnerable tend to direct frustration-produced aggression inward against the self, and have a history of faulty and tenuous interpersonal relationships.

(2) The more central the frustration is to the heart of the personality, the more intense the frustration, and therefore the more severe will be its aftermath. The loss of a lover is more difficult to adjust to than an arbitrary insult at the hands of a stranger.

(3) The social context in which a person is embedded may make certain patterns of interpersonal frustrations more likely. Some cultures have a greater number of thwarting-disorientation situations, to use Naroll's terms, than others. Societies high in interpersonal frustration, all other things being equal, will have

higher rates of suicide.

(4) Societies also vary in the extent to which they provide close, meaningful, and relatively conflict-free interactions among their members. Cultures which provide such positive interpersonal milieus will have, all things being equal, low rates of suicide.

Theoretically a calculus of suicide might be constructed, such that the likelihood of suicide or a society's rate of suicide is a function of the values assigned to each of the following variables: (1) personal vulnerability to interpersonal frustration, (2) the intensity of such frustration, (3) the likelihood of experiencing such frustration in a social framework, and (4) the likelihood of support and the extent to which that support is provided to the individual by the social framework.

Each of these factors is examined, for example, by Jacobs (31) in his lucid description of the network and succession of interpersonal frustrations which are common to the life histories of American adolescents who commit suicide. His presentation illustrates how, intuitively and independently, investigators have focused on the social and personal aspects of interpersonal frustration as antecedents to suicide.

Based upon an analysis of the case histories, Jacobs derived the following central hypothesis:

> Adolescent suicide attempts result from the adolescent feeling that he has been subject to a progressive isolation from meaningful social relationships. The formal aspects of this process are outlined below. The adolescent must have experienced:
> 1. A long-standing history of problems (from early childhood to onset of adolescence).
> 2. The escalation of problems (since the onset of adolescence) above and beyond those usually associated with adolescence.
> 3. The progressive failure of available adaptive techniques

for coping with the old and new increasing problems which leads to the adolescent's progressive isolation from meaningful social relationships.

4. A chain reaction dissolution of any remaining meaningful social relationships in the days and weeks preceding the attempt which leads to the adolescent's feeling that he has reached "the end of hope."

5. The internal process by which he justifies suicide to himself, and thus manages to bridge the gap between thought and process.

As comprehensive as this may appear, Jacobs neglects to give proper emphasis to the macrosocial aspects of suicide in our culture in particular, and other cultures in general. Not all societies treat adolescents as roughly as our own. To round out this picture, one may turn to Erikson's work. In a very real sense, Erickson's schema of developmental crises (14) depicts a number of major structural foci for potentially intense interpersonal frustrations in American society. For example, Erikson's description of the manner in which the identity crisis came to his attention highlights its psychosocial significance and causation:

We begin to conceptualize matters of identity at the very time in history when they become a problem. For we do so in a country which attempts to make a super-identity out of all the identities imported by its constituent immigrants; and we do so at a time when rapidly increasing industrialization threatens these essentially agrarian and patrician identities in their lands of origin as well.

The study of identity, then, becomes as strategic in our own time as the study of sexuality was in Freud's time. Such historical relativity in the development of a field, however, does not seem to preclude consistency of ground plan and continued closeness to observable fact. Freud's findings regarding sexual etiology of a mental disturbance are as true for our patients as they were for his; while the burden of identity which stands out in our considerations probably burdened Freud's patients as well as ours, as re-interpretations would show. Different periods thus permit us to see in temporary exaggeration different aspects of an essentially inseparable whole.

IMPLICATIONS FOR THE PREVENTION OF SUICIDE

Because suicide seems to result from a disruption in interpersonal relationships, the immediate therapeutic task in dealing with suicidal individuals is to aid them in reconstituting old, and forming new close, reliable, and relatively stress-free ties with others. This is a formidable undertaking, especially since some suicidal individuals have had little experience with wholesome and normal relationships, while others feel that they are unworthy of redemption. The intense ambivalence which often characterizes attitudes toward suicide often makes matters even more difficult.

No matter how successful the individual or group treatment of potentially suicidal individuals is, it is unlikely to reduce a culture's rate of suicide, as has been demonstrated for our culture by Maris (39).

Suicide will be with us as long as societies pose threats crucial to the social relationships of its culture-bearers, and do not provide them with the wherewithal to survive such threats successfully. To reduce the rate of suicide in a society, one must first reform that society.

REFERENCES

1. Aron, R. *Main Currents of Sociological Thought,* Vol. 2. New York: Anchor, 1970.

2. Akiskal, H.S., and McKinney, W.T. "Depressive Disorders: Toward a Unified Hypothesis," *Science* 182 (1963), 20-29.

3. Berkowitz, L. (Ed.) *Roots of Aggression.* New York: Atherton, 1969.

4. Bogoras, W. The Chukchee. In F. Boas (Ed.), "The Jesup North Pacific Expedition," *Memoirs of the American Museum of Natural History* 7 (1909), 560.

5. Bovard, E.W. "The Effects of Social Stimuli on the Response to Stress," *Psychological Review* 66 (1959), 267-77.

6. Camus, A. *The Myth of Sisyphus.* New York: Vintage, 1953.

7. Cohen, E.A. *Human Behavior in the Concentration Camp.* New York: Grosset & Dunlap, 1953.

8. Dickinson, E. "I felt a funeral in my brain," *Complete Poems of Emily Dickinson.* Boston: Little, Brown, 1960.

9. Dollard, J., Doob, L.W., Miller, N.E., Mowrer, O.H., and Sears, R.R. *Frustration and Aggression.* New Haven: Yale University Press, 1939.

10. Douglas, J. *The Social Meaning of Suicide.* Princeton: Princeton University Press, 1967.

11. Durkheim, E. *Suicide.* Glencoe, Ill.: Free Press, 1951.

12. Erikson, E.H. "Autobiographical Notes on the Identity Crises," *Daedalus,* 99 (1970), 730-59.

13. ———.*Childhood and Society.* New York: Norton, 1950.

14. ———. *Identity: Youth and Crisis.* New York: Norton, 1968.

15. Freud, S. *Beyond the Pleasure Principle.* New York: Bantam, 1959.

16. ———. Letter to Martha Bernays, September 16, 1883. In E.L. Freud (Ed.), *The Letters of Sigmund Freud.* New York: McGraw Hill, 1960.

17. ———. "Mourning and Melancholia," *Collected Papers of Sigmund Freud,* Vol. 4. London: Hogarth, 1956.

18. ———. On Narcissism: an Introduction. In J. Strachey (Ed.), *The Complete Psychological Works of Sigmund Freud,* Vol. 12. London: Hogarth, 1962.

19. ———.Psycho-analytical Notes on an Autobiographical Account of Paranoia (Dementia Paranoides). In J. Strachey (Ed.), *The Complete Psychological works of Sigmund Freud,* Vol. 12. London: Hogarth, 1962.

20. ———. The Economic Problems of Masochism. In J. Strachey (Ed.), *The Complete Psychological Works of Sigmund Freud,* Vol. 12. London: Hogarth, 1962

21. Futterman, S. "Suicide: Psychoanalytic Point of View." In N.L. Farberow and E.S. Shneidman (Eds.). *The Cry for Help.* New York: McGraw-Hill, 1961, 168-180.

22. Gibbs, J.P., and Martin, W. *Status Integration and Suicide.*   Eugene, Oregon: University of Oregon Press, 1964.

23. Goodwin, G. *The Social Organization of the Western Apache.* Chicago: University of Chicago Press, 1942.

24. Hattem, J.V. *The Precipitating   Role of Discordant Interpersonal Relationships in Suicidal Behavior.* Ann Arbor University Microfilms 64-6303, 1964.

25. Hendin, H. *Suicide and Scandinavia.* New York: Grune & Stratton, 1964.

26. Henry, A.F. and Short, J.F. *Suicide and Homicide.* Glencoe, Ill.: Free Press, 1954.

27. Hesse, H. *Steppenwolf.* New York: Bantam, 1963.

28. Hoebel, E.A. *The Cheyennes.* New York: Holt, 1960.

29. Hsu, F.L.K. *Americans and Chinese.* Garden City, N.Y.: Natural History Press, 1953.

30. ———. "American Core Value and National Character." In F.L.K. Hsu (Ed.), *Psychological Anthropology.* Cambridge, Mass., 1972, 241-266.

31. Jacobs, J. *Adolescent Suicide.* New York: Wiley, 1971.

32. Jones, E. *The Life and Work of Sigmund Freud.* New York: Basic Books, 1957.

33. Krauss, H.H. *A Cross-cultural Study of Suicide.* Unpublished doctoral dissertation, Northwestern University, 1966.

34. Krauss, H.H. & Krauss, B.J. "A Cross-cultural Study of the Thwarting Disorientation Theory of Suicide," *Journal of Abnormal Psychology* 73 (1968), 353-57.

35. La Capra, D. *Emile Durkheim, Sociologist and Philosopher.* Ithaca, N.Y.: Cornell University Press, 1972.

36. Lecky, P. *Self-consistency: A Theory of Personality.* Garden City, N.Y.: Doubleday, 1969.

37. Lewin, K. *A Dynamic Theory of Personality.* New York: McGraw-Hill, 1953.

38. Malinowski, B. *Crime and Custom in Savage Society.* Patterson, N.J.: Littlefield, Adams and Co., 1964.

39. Maris, R.W. "The Sociology of Suicide Prevention: Policy Implications of Differences between Suicidal Patients and Completed Suicides," *Social Problems* 17 (1969), 132-49.

40. Mead, G.H. *Mind, Self and Society from the Standpoint of a Social Behaviorist.* Chicago: University of Chicago Press, 1934.

41. Meerloo, J.A. *Suicide and Mass Suicide.* New York: Grune & Stratton, 1962.

42. Menninger, K. *Man Against Himself.* New York: Harcourt, Brace and World, 1938.

43. ———. *The Vital Balance.* New York: Viking, 1963.

44. Merton, R.K. *Social Theory and Social Structure.* New York: Free Press, 1957.

45. Naroll, R. *Data Quality Control.* New York: Free Press, 1962.

46. ———. Cultural Determinants and the Concept of the Sick Society. In S.C. Plog and R.B. Edgerton (Eds.), *Changing Perspectives in Mental Illness.* New York: Holt, Rinehart & Winston, 1969, 128-55.

47. Opler, V.K. Cultural Induction of Stress. In M.H. Appley & R. Trumbull (Eds.), *Psychological Stress.* New York: Appleton-Century-Crofts, 1967, 209-41.

48. Powell, E.H. "Occupation, Status and Suicide: Toward a Redefinition of Anomie," *American Sociological Review 23* (1958), 131-39.

49. Schur, M. *Freud:Living and Dying.* New York: International Universities Press, 1972.

50. Sears, R.R. Attachment, Dependency, and Frustration. In J.L. Gerwirtz (Ed.), *Attachment and Dependency.* Washington: Winston, 1972, 1-27.

51. Seligman, C.S. and Seligman, B.Z. "The Kababish, a Sudan Arab tribe," *Harvard African Studies 2* (1918), 105-86.

52. Simmel, G. "The Sociology of Sociability," *American Journal of Sociology* 55 (1949), 254-61.

53. Simpson, G. "Methodological Problems in Determining the Aetiology of Suicide," *American Sociological Review* 15 (1950), 658-63.

54. Sullivan, H.S. *Conceptions of Modern Psychiatry.* New York: Norton, 1940.

55. Tabachnik, V., Litman, R.E., Osman, M., Jones, W.L., Cohn, J., Kaspar, A., and Moffat, J. "Comparative Psychiatric Study of Accidental and Suicidal Death," *Archives of General Psychiatry* 14(1966), 60-68.

56. Zimmer, H. *The Philosophies of India.* New York: Meridian, 1956.

III

On Death and The Continuity of Life: A "New" Paradigm

ROBERT JAY LIFTON

SERIOUS CONCERN WITH THE WAY IN WHICH PEOPLE CONFRONT death leads one to question the nature of death, and the nature of life in the face of death. In my work in Hiroshima I found that studying an extreme situation such as that facing the survivors of the atomic bomb can lead to insights about everyday death, about ordinary people facing what Kurt Vonnegut has called "plain old death." I feel that our psychological ideas about death have been so stereotyped, so limited, so extraordinarily impoverished, that any exposure to a holocaust like Hiroshima, or My Lai, or in fact the entire American involvement in Indochina, forces us to develop new ideas and hypotheses that begin to account for some of the reactions that we observe. I want to suggest a few such principles that are both psychological and historical.

My basic premise is that we understand man through paradigms or models. The choice of the paradigm or model becomes extremely important, because it determines what might be called the "controlling image" or central theme of our psychological theory. Human culture is sufficiently rich that a great variety of paradigms are available to serve as controlling images, including those of "power," "being," "instinct and defense," "social class," "collective unconscious," "interpersonal relations," and so on. These paradigms are by no means of equal merit, but each can be used to illuminate some aspect of human experience.

At the end of my study of Hiroshima, *Death In Life,* I stated that sexuality and moralism had been the central themes confronted by Freud in developing psychoanalysis, but that now unlimited technological violence and absurd death have become more pressing themes for contemporary man (1). During the Victorian era, when Freud was evolving his ideas, there was an overwhelming repression of sexuality, but a relatively greater openness to the reality of human death. The extent of sexual repression is revealed by the Victorian custom of putting doilies on table legs, because they were thought to be suggestive of human anatomy. There has been a historical shift, and the contemporary situation is one in which we are less overwhelmed by sexual difficulties but more overwhelmed by difficulties about death. We have shifted from covering the legs of tables with doilies to wearing hotpants; on the other hand, the Grim Reaper is no longer a public celebrity. Instead we bury him in the Forest Lawn syndrome.

The fact that Freud's model of libido and repression of instinctual sexual impulses was put forth during the late Victorian era, at a time when society was struggling with these issues, does not invalidate the generalizability of his ideas: their power lies precisely in that generalizability. But it does raise the important point, not only for Freud but for our own work now, of the influence of historical forces on the psychological theories we choose to develop. If we now begin to center psychological theory around death, it is because death imposes itself upon us in such unmanageable ways.

In my psychological work on extreme historical situations involving ultimate violence and massive death, I have preferred to speak of a process of psychic numbing rather than of repression. Repression occurs when an idea or experience is forgotten, excluded from consciousness, or relegated to the realm of the unconscious. Repressed childhood memories and repressed instinctual impulses are illustrations of this process. Repression is part of a model or controlling image characterized by drives and defenses, and refers to the compensatory effort of the organism to cope with innate or instinctual forces that dominate emotional life. The original idea was to analyze these forces and thereby bring the patient to a cure.

Psychoanalysis has been changed significantly by the development of ego psychology, by various neo-Freudian modifications, and by many new influences, including ethology. But I think that psychoanalytic theory is still bedeviled by its traditional imagery of instinct, repression, and defense. This imagery yields limited and distorted insight into the subject of death, and also into the relationship of death to larger contemporary experience. The concept of psychic numbing, in contrast, suggests the cessation of what I call the formative process, the impairment of man's essential mental function of symbol formation or symbolization. This point of view is strongly influenced by the symbolic philosophy of Cassirer and Langer (2). Psychic numbing is a form of desensitization; it refers to an incapacity to feel or to confront certain kinds of experience, due to the blocking or absence of inner forms or imagery that can connect with such experience.

The importance of this kind of phenomenon has been impressed upon me very profoundly. It would appear that the technology of destruction has had a strong impact on the spread of psychic numbing. But my assumption is that psychic numbing is central in everyday experience as well, and may be identified whenever there is interference in the "formative" mental function, the process of creating viable inner forms. The "psychoformative" perspective stresses that a human being can never simply receive a bit of naked information. The process of perception is vitally bound up with the process of inner recreation, in which one utilizes whatever forms are available in individual psychic existence.

Within this psychoformative perspective, the central paradigm I wish to develop is that of *death and the continuity of life.* In elaborating this paradigm I will speak first of a theory of symbolic immortality, then of an accompanying theory of evolving death imagery, and finally discuss the application of this paradigm in clinical work and psychopathology.

I want to emphasize at the beginning that this approach to psychology and history is impelled by a sense of urgency about our present historical predicament, and by a strong desire to evolve psychohistorical theory adequate to the dangerous times in which we live. In this approach it is necessary to make our own subjectivity as investigators clear and conscious, to try to understand it, and to use it as part of the conceptual process. I have elsewhere suggested possibilities for going even further, and making our forms of advocacy clear, forthright, and, again, part of the conceptual process (3). In presenting this paradigm of death and the continuity of life, I also assume a sense of urgency in our intellectual and professional lives. A crisis exists in the psychiatric profession, and in other professions as well, that has to do with despair about the adequacy of traditional ideas for coping with new data impinging from all sides.

In his book, *The Structure of Scientific Revolutions* (4), Thomas Kuhn describes a sequence that occurs in the development of scientific thought when the data can no longer be explained by prevailing theories. Kuhn observed that when this happens the usual reaction among scientists is to cling to the old theories all the more persistently. At a certain point the incongruity between the theory and data becomes so glaring—and the anxiety of those defending the theory so great—that the whole system collapses and the paradigm changes. I think we are at a point like that now, and that a new depth-psychological paradigm is required.

Psychiatrists and psychoanalysts have for the most part left the question of death to philosophers. Freud's theory legitimized this neglect when he said (5):

It is indeed impossible to imagine our own death: and whenever we attempt to do so we can perceive that we are in fact still present as spectators. Hence the psychoanalytic school could venture on the assertion that at bottom no one believes in his own death, or to put the same thing in another way, that in his unconscious, every one of us is convinced of his own immortality.

Freud viewed all interest in imortality as compensatory, as a denial of death and a refusal to face it unflinchingly. Freud insisted that we look at death squarely, that we cannot psychologically afford the consequences of denial. But Freud had no place in his system for the *symbolic* significance of the idea of immortality as an expression of continuity. For this reason we may call Freud's approach "rationalist-iconoclastic."

Jung's approach was very different; he took the mythological and symbolic aspects of death and immortality very seriously. He emphasized the enormous significance of the idea of immortality on the basis of the map of the human psyche, and especially of the unconscious, that is provided by mythology. He also said: "As a physician I am convinced that it is hygienic to discover in death a goal toward which one can strive: and that shrinking away from it is something unhealthy and abnormal." And, "I...consider the religious teaching of a life hereafter consonant with the standpoint of psychic hygiene" (6). It is unclear here whether Jung is talking about the literal idea of a life after death, or a more symbolic one. He surrenders much of the scientific viewpoint, however broadly defined, that man has struggled for so painfully over the last few centuries. We can thus call Jung's approach "hygienic-mythical."

Both of these views are important; neither is completely satisfactory. Freud's attitude has the merit of unflinching acceptance of death as a total annihilation of the organism. Jung's view has the merit of stressing the symbolic significance of universal imagery around death and immortality.

A third perspective—a "formative-symbolic" view—draws upon both Freud and Jung, but takes into account the increasing awareness of symbol formation as a fundamental characteristic of man's psychic life. I should emphasize that I am speaking of an ongoing process of symbolization, rather than of particular symbols like the flag, or the cross. In classical psychoanalysis the focus tends to be in symbols as specific equivalents—pencil for penis, sea for mother—and much less upon the more fundamental process of creation and recreation of images and forms that characterize human mentation.

I would hold, in the context of this psychoformative view, that even in our unconscious lives we are by no means convinced of our own immortality. Rather we have what some recent workers have called "middle knowledge" (7) of the idea of death. We both "know" that we will die, and resist and fail to act upon that knowledge. Nor is the need to transcend death mere denial. More essentially, it represents a compelling universal urge to maintain an inner sense of continuous symbolic relationship, over time and space, with the various elements of life. In other words, I am speaking of a sense of immortality as in itself neither compensatory nor pathological, but as man's symbolization of his ties with both his biological fellows and his history, past and future. This view is consistent with Otto Rank's stress on man's perpetual need for "an assurance of eternal survival of his self." Rank suggested that "man creates culture by changing natural conditions in order to maintain his spiritual self" (8). But this need for a sense of symbolic immortality, interwoven with man's biology and his history, is for the most part ignored by individually-biased psychological theory.

The sense of immortality can be expressed in five general modes. The first and most obvious is the biological mode, the sense of living on through and in one's sons and daughters and their sons and daughters. At some level of consciousness we imagine an endless chain of biological attachments. This mode has been a classical expression of symbolic immortality in East Asian culture, especially in traditional China, with its extraordinary emphasis on the family line. In Confucian ethics, the greatest of all unfilial acts is lack of posterity. But this mode never remains purely biological: it becomes simultaneously biosocial, and expresses itself in attachments to one's group, tribe, organization, people, nation, or even species. Ultimately one can feel at least glimmerings of a sense of immortality in living on through and in mankind.

A second expression of the sense of immortality is the theological idea of a life after death, or, more importantly, the idea of release from profane life to existence on a higher plane. The literal idea of an afterlife is not essential to this mode, and such a notion is not present in many religions. More basic is the concept of transcending death through spiritual attainment. The power of spiritual life to in some way overcome death is exemplified in all the great religious leaders around whom religions have been founded: Buddha, Moses, Christ, Mohammed. Within each of the religious traditions there has been a word to convey the spiritual state in which one has transcended death: the Japanese *kami*; the Polynesian *mana*; the Roman idea of *noumen*; the Eskimo concept of *tungnik*; and the Christian doctrine of *grace*. All these words describe a state in which one possesses spiritual power over death, meaning, in a symbolic sense, that one is in harmony with a principle extending beyond the limited biological life span.

The third mode of symbolic immortality is that achieved through works—the mode of creativity, the achievement of enduring human impact. It is the sense that one's writing, one's teaching, one's human influences, great or humble, will live on; that one's contribution will not die. The therapeutic efforts of physicians and psychotherapists are strongly impelled, I believe, by an image of therapeutic impact extending through the patient to others, including the patient's children, in an endless potentially beneficent chain of influence. The "therapeutic despair" described so sensitively by Leslie Farber (9) as an occupational hazard of the psychiatrist treating schizophrenic patients may well result from the perception that one's strenuous therapeutic endeavors are not producing these lasting effects, and that one's energies are not animating the life of the patient and cannot therefore symbolically extend the life of the therapist.

A fourth mode is the sense of immortality achieved through being survived by nature itself: the theme of eternal nature. This theme is very vivid among the Japanese, and was one of the most important kinds of imagery for survivors of the atomic bomb. It is strong not only in Shinto belief, but in the European Romantic movement, and in the Anglo Saxon cult of the great outdoors—indeed, it exists in every culture in one form or another.

The fifth mode is somewhat different from the others in that it depends solely upon a psychic state. This is the state of "experiential transcendence," a state so intense that in it time and death disappear. When one achieves ecstasy or rapture, the restrictions of the senses—including the sense of mortality—no longer exist. Poetically and religiously this has been described as "losing oneself." It can occur not only in religious or secular mysticism, but also in song, dance, battle, sexual love, childbirth, athletic effort, mechanical flight, or while contemplating works of artistic or intellectual creation (10). This state is characterized by extra-ordinary psychic unity and perceptual intensity. But there also occurs, as we hear described in drug experiences, a process of symbolic reordering. One feels oneself to be different after returning from this state. I see experiential transcendence and its aftermath as epitomizing the death-and-rebirth experience. It is central to change or transformation, and has great significance for psychotherapy. Experiential transcendence includes a feeling of what Eliade has called "continuous present" that can be equated with eternity or with "mythical time" (11). This continuous present is perceived as not only here and now, but as inseparable from past and future.

The theory of symbolic immortality can be used to illuminate changes in cultural emphasis from one historical period to another. We can think of historical shifts as involving alterations in the stress given to one or another mode or combinations of modes. The Darwinian revolution of the nineteenth century, for example, can be seen as entailing a shift from a predominantly theological mode to a more natural and biological one. The continuous transformation in China over the last few decades involves a shift from a family-centered biological mode to a revolutionary mode, which as I have said elsewhere, emphasizes man's works but also includes elements of other modes with periodic emphasis upon experiential transcendence.

Following the holocaust of World War II, the viability of psychic activity within the modes has undergone something of a collapse, at least in the West. We exist now in a time of doubt about modes of continuity and connection, and I believe this has direct relevance for work with individual patients. Awareness of our historical predicament—of threats posed by nuclear weapons, environmental destruction, and the press of rising population against limited resources—has created extensive imagery of extinction. These threats occur at a time when the rate of historical velocity and the resulting psychohistorical dislocation had already undermined established symbols around the institutions of family, church, government, and education. Combined imagery of extinction and dislocation leave us in doubt about whether we will live on in our children and their children, in our groups and organizations, in our works, in our spirituality, or even in nature, which we now know to be vulnerable to our pollutions and our weaponry. It is the loss of faith, I think, in these four modes of symbolic immortality that leads people, especially the young, to plunge—sometimes desperately and sometimes with considerable self-realization—into the mode of experiential transcendence. This very old and classical form of personal quest has had to be discovered anew in the face of doubts about the other four modes.

In postulating a theory of symbolic immortality on such a grand scale, one must also account for the everyday idea of death, for the sense of *mortality* that develops over the course of a lifetime. Freud's notion of the death instinct is unacceptable, and could, in fact, be viewed as a contradiction in terms in that instinctual forces are in the service of the preservation of life. Nor is death an adequate goal for life. Yet—as is generally the case with Freud when we disagree with him—the concept, whatever its confusions around the instinctual idiom, contains an insight we had best retain concerning the fundamental importance of death for psychological life. Hence, the widespread rejection of the death instinct poses the danger not so much of throwing out the baby with the bath water, as of discarding the grim reaper along with the scythe.

Freud himself faced death heroically and understood well the dangers involved in denying man's mortality. But at the same time, Freudian theory, by insisting that death has no representation in the unconscious, has relegated fear of death to a derivative of fear of castration. Freud also seemed ambivalent about whether to view death and life within a unitary or dualistic perspective. His ultimate instinctual dualism opposed death and life instinct. Yet the notion of life leading inevitably toward death is a unitary vision, and it is this unitary element that I think we should preserve. This unitary perspective on death would insist upon its over-all consistency as an absolute infringement upon the organism (as opposed to certain contemporary efforts to subdivide death into a number of different categories); and as an event anticipated, and therefore influential, from the beginning of the life of the organism.

I believe that the representation of death evolves from dim and vague articulation in the young organism's inchoate imagery to sophisticated symbolization in maturity. I rely partly here on Kenneth Boulding's work on the image (13), in which he has stressed the presence in the organism from the very beginning of some innate tendency or direction—what I call here *inchoate image*. This inchoate image is at first simply a direction or physiological push. But inchoate though it may be, the image includes an interpretative anticipation of interaction with the environment. Evidence for the existence of innate imagery can be drawn from two sources: one is ethology, and the other is observation of rapid eyeball movements (REM) in sleep studies.

Work in ethology has demonstrated through the study of "releasing mechanisms" the existence of what I am here calling an image. The newborn organism is impelled innately toward certain expected behavior on the part of older (nurturing) organisms, which when encountered acts as a releasing mechanism for a specific action (such as feeding) of its own. Sleep studies also suggest the presence of images in some form from the beginning of life, possibly during prenatal experience, that "cause," or at least provide some basis for, the rapid eyeball movements observed in various species. Rather than demonstrating the presence of pictorial images, these two areas of research suggest the presence at birth of primordial images or precursors to later imagery.

In the human being, the sequence of this process is from physiological push (or direction of the organism), to pictures of the world (images in the usual sense), to symbolization. This theory of evolving imagery explains the elaboration of the inner idea of death from earliest childhood in terms of three subparadigms or polarities. These are: connection versus separation; integrity versus disintegration; and movement versus stasis. The inchoate imagery of the first polarity is expressed in a seeking of connection, what John Bowlby has described as "attachment behavior" around sucking, clinging, smiling, crying, and following (14). The organism actively seeks connection with the nurturing or mothering person. First this quest is mainly physiological, then is internalized in pictorial image formation, and finally becomes highly symbolized. The organism's evolution is from simple movement toward the mother to a nurturing relationship with her, and eventually toward connection with the other people, with groups, with ideas, and with historical forces. Where this striving for connection fails, as it always must in some degree, there is the alternative image of separation, of being cut off. This alternative image of separation forms one precursor for the idea of death.

We can look at the idea of integrity versus disintegration in a similar way. As indicated in the work of Melanie Klein on the infant's fear of annihilation (15), there is from the beginning some sense of the organism's being threatened with dissolution and disintegration. The terms of this negative image or fear are at first entirely physiological, having to do with physical intactness or deterioration; but over the course of time, integrity, without entirely losing its physiological reference, comes to assume primarily ethical-psychological dimensions. At those more symbolized levels, one "disintegrates" as one's inner forms and images become inadequate representations of the self-world relationship, and inadequate bases for action.

The third mode, that of movement versus stasis, is the most ignored of the three, but it has great clinical significance and is especially vivid to those who deal with children. An infant held tight and unable to move becomes extremely anxious and uncomfortable. The early meaning of movement is the literal, physiological idea of moving the body or a portion of it from one place to another. Later the meaning of movement takes on symbolic qualities having to do with development, progress, and change (or with a specific collectivity in some form of motion). The absence of movement becomes a form of stasis, a deathlike experience closely related to psychic numbing.

One could illustrate in detail the evolution of these polarities over the course of the life cycle. But it is clear that rather early, or earlier than is usually assumed, death achieves some kind of conscious meaning. By the age of three, four, and five, children are thinking and talking, however confusedly, about death and dying. And over the course of the next few years something in that process consolidates so that the idea of death is more fundamentally learned and understood. At every developmental level all conflicts exacerbate, and are exacerbated by, these three aspects of what later becomes death anxiety—that is, disintegration, stasis, or separation. These death-linked conflicts take on characteristic form for each developmental stage, and reach a climax during adolescence.

During young adulthood there occurs a process partly described by Kenneth Keniston around the term "youth" (16), and partly described in my own work around the concept of the "protean style" (17). I see the continuing search that characterizes the protean style as a constant process of death and rebirth of inner form. The quest is always for images and forms more malleable and inwardly acceptable at this historical moment than those available from the past. Sometime in early adulthood one moves more fully into the realm of historical action, and then one connects with the modes of symbolic immortality.

Later, in middle adulthood, one becomes impressed that one will indeed die. It becomes apparent that the limitations of physiology and life span will not permit the full accomplishment of all one's projects. But even with the fuller recognition of mortality, the issues of integrity, connection, and movement remain salient. Old people approaching death look back nostalgically over their whole lives. This life review, as it is sometimes called, has to do with a process of self-judgment, of examining one's life around issues of integrity, but also of connection and movement; and of looking for evidence of relationship to the modes of symbolic immortality.

How do these principles apply in mental disturbance? I want to suggest the clinical applicability of this paradigm of death, and the continuity of life for various categories of psychopathology. Psychiatrists have turned away from death, as has our whole culture, and there has been little appreciation of the importance of death anxiety in the precipitation of psychological disorder.

What I am here calling the sense of immortality is close to what Erik Erikson calls basic trust (18). Erikson emphasizes the issue of basic trust as the earliest developmental crisis, and he sees the legacy of this earliest time as having vital importance for adulthood. But the establishment of trust itself involves confidence in the integrity, connection, and movement of life, prerequisites for a viable form of symbolic immortality. Where this confidence collapses, psychological impairment ensues.

The principle of impaired death imagery—or more accurately, of impaired imagery of death and the continuity of life—is a unitary theme around which mental illness can be described and in some degree understood. I see this kind of impairment as being involved in the ethology of mental illness, but not as causative—in the nineteenth-century sense of a single cause bringing about one specific effect. Rather, impaired death imagery is at the center of a constellation of forms, each of which is of some importance for the over-all process we call mental disturbance. Here I would point to three relevant issues central to the process of mental illness. The first is death anxiety, which evolves in relation to the three polarities I have described. The second is psychic numbing, which I see as a process of desymbolization and deformation. The image which accompanies psychic numbing is that "If I feel nothing, then death does not exist. Therefore I need not feel anxious about death, either actually or symbolically; I am invulnerable." A third principle is what I call "suspicion of counterfeit nurturance." This is the idea that if death exists, then life is counterfeit. Ionesco's question— "Why was I born if it wasn't forever?"—illustrates the relation of this theme to the quest for immortality. But it is a very old question.

Death anxiety can be seen as a signal of threat to the organism, a threat that is understood as disintegration, stasis, or separation. All anxiety relates to these equivalents of death imagery; guilt, too, is generated insofar as one makes oneself "responsible" for these processes. In other writing I have distinguished between static (either numbed or self-lacerating) and animating guilt, and have emphasized the importance of the latter in the process of self-transformation (19).

One can take as a model for much of neurosis the syndrome which used to be called "traumatic neurosis" or "war neurosis." It is generally described as involving the continuous reliving of the unconscious conflicts aroused by the traumatic situation. More recently, emphasis has been placed on imagery of death aroused by the trauma, rather than the trauma *per se*. Thus the syndrome has been called by some observers "death anxiety neurosis" (20). I see this process in terms of the psychology of the survivor, as I have elaborated that psychology in my work on Hiroshima and more recently with antiwar veterans.

My belief is that survivor conflicts emerge from and apply to everyday psychological experience as well. When one "outlives" something or someone, and there are of course many large and small survivals in anyone's life, the specter of premature death becomes vivid. Simultaneously one begins to feel what I have called "guilt over survival priority"—the notion that one's life was purchased at the cost of another's, that one was able to survive *because* someone else died. This is a classical survivor process, and is very much involved in traumatic neurosis. In describing traumatic neurosis, earlier observers spoke of "ego contraction" (21). This is close to what I call psychic numbing, also very marked in the survivor syndrome and in neurosis in general.

A great number of writers (including Stekel, Rank, Horney, and Tillich) have emphasized patterns closely resembling psychic numbing as the essence of neurosis. Stekel, in 1908, spoke of neurotics who "die every day" and who "play the game of dying" (22). Otto Rank referred to the neurotic's "constant restriction of life" because "he refuses the loan (life) in order to avoid the payment of the debt (death)" (23). The neurotic thus seeks to defend himself against stimuli in a way that Freud described in a little-known passage in *Civilization and Its Discontents.* Freud observed (24);

No matter how much we may shrink with horror from certain situations—of a galley slave in antiquity, of a peasant during the Thirty Years War, of a victim of the Holy Inquisition, of a Jew awaiting a pogrom—it is nevertheless impossible for us to feel our way into such people, to divine the changes which original obtuseness of mind, a gradual stupefying process, the cessation of expectations and cruder or more refined methods of narcotization have produced upon their receptivity to sensations of pleasure and unpleasure. Moreover, in the case of the most extreme possibility of suffering, special mental protective devices are brought into operation.

It is strange that Freud turned away from his own argument at this point and concluded that it was "unprofitable to pursue this aspect of the problem any further." For the argument contained the core of the idea of psychic numbing in extreme situations. The holocausts described by Freud have become almost a norm, a model of our times. But in lesser degree, what Freud called narcotization and I am calling psychic numbing is associated with the individual holocausts and survivals around which neurosis takes shape.

Let me now make some preliminary suggestions from a work in progress (25) about the significance of these struggles around death imagery for the classical psychiatric syndromes. If we view neurosis in general as an expression of psychic numbing—shrinking of the ego and diminished capacity for experience—we can see in depression specific examples of impaired mourning, impaired symbolization, and the impaired formulation of the survivor. Where a known loss triggers the process, as in reactive depression, the depressed person acts very much like a survivor, and psychic numbing becomes very prominent. He often expresses the feeling that a part of him has died, and that he "killed" the other person in some symbolic way by failing to sustain the other's life with needed support, help, and nurturance. The idea of either having killed the other person, or of having purchased one's own life at the cost of another person's is fundamental. Such feelings are also related to Freud's explanation of guilt, in that earlier ambivalent feelings toward the other person included hate and death wishes, which now become attached to the actual loss. Grief is of enormous importance in the experience of survival, and in its residuum of mental physical disturbance is related to psychic numbing.

In character disorders, and in the related phenomenon of

psychosomatic disorders in which one speaks through the language of the body, there are lifelong characterological patterns of deadening or numbing of various aspects of the psyche. This numbing may involve moral sensitivity or interpersonal capacities. However the numbing is expressed, there is a situation of meaninglessness and unfulfilled life, in which the defensive psychological structures built up to ward off death anxiety also ward off autonomy and self-understanding.

As for hysteria, the "psychic anesthesia" emphasized in the early literature suggests the centrality of stasis, deadening, or numbing. Freud's case of Anna O., for example, is properly understood as a mourning reaction (26). The hysteria followed very quickly upon the death of Anna's father, and had much to do with her reaction to that death. Her conception of being alive became altered in such a way that merely to live and feel—to exist as a sexual being—was dangerous, impermissable, and a violation of an unspoken pact with the dead person. Whether or not there is a mourning reaction directly involved, hysteria tends to involve either this form of stasis or its seeming opposite, exaggerated movement or activity that serves as a similar barrier against feeling and living. These patterns again resemble those among Hiroshima survivors.

In obsessional neurosis and obsessive-compulsive styles of behavior the stress is upon order and control. One tries to "stop time," to control its flow so as to order existence and block spontaneous expression, which is in turn felt to be threatening and "deadly."

Much of Freudian theory of phobia evolved from the history of Little Hans. Freud's interpretation of this case was that Hans' castration fears were displaced and transformed into a fear of horses—that is, the inner danger was transformed into an external one (27). But Little Hans' experience may also be understood in terms of fear of annihilation and separation. His castration fear epitomized, but was not the cause of, his general death anxiety. Rather than viewing this death anxiety as secondary to castration anxiety, as psychoanalytic literature has done ever since, we do better to reverse our understanding and interpret the castration anxiety as an expression of more general death anxiety.

Finally I want to turn to psychosis and to an application of this theoretical position to schizophrenia. It is appalling to consider the degree to which death imagery has been observed in schizophrenic persons without being incorporated into any conceptual scheme. As with more general psychiatric concern with death, the situation is changing. Harold Searles (28) writes at some length about the problems that the schizophrenic person has with the "universal factor of mortality." Searles says that the schizophrenic patient doesn't really believe he is living, doesn't feel himself to be alive, feels life is passing him by, and feels stalked by death. Thus the patient employs a variety of techniques to defend himself against death anxiety, and yet in another sense feels himself already dead, "having therefore nothing to lose through death."

What Ronald Laing calls the "false self" is very close to what I am calling a numbed or "dead self." Laing "translates" from what he calls "schizophrenese"; he describes "the desire to be dead, the desire for a non-being" as "perhaps the most dangerous desire that can be pursued"; and the "state of death-in-life" as both a response to "the primary guilt of having no right to life in the first place, and hence of being entitled at most only to a dead life" and "probably the most extreme defensive posture that can be adopted," in which "being dead, one cannot die, and one cannot kill" (29). What Searles and Laing describe in schizophrenics is reminiscent of the process observable among survivors in Hiroshima; it is also similar to the *Musselmanner* phenomenon that occurred in Nazi concentration camps, where the state of psychic numbing was so extreme that, as one observer put it, "One hesitates to call their death death" (30). These were people who had become robots.

The schizophrenic experiences a pathetic illusion of omnipotence, a despairing mask of pseudo-immortality because he is blocked in the most fundamental way from authentic connection or continuity—from the sense of symbolic immortality. But the productions of the schizophrenic are infused with death: again like the Hiroshima survivors at the time the bomb fell, he sees himself as dead, other people around him as dead, the world as dead.

Wynne, Lidz, and others who have studied family process in schizophrenia emphasize the transmission of "meaninglessness, pointlessness, and emptiness," of "irrationality," of "schism and skew" (31). Bateson's double bind theory of conflicted messages received by the child also stresses the difficulty faced by the child in establishing a coherent field of meaning (32). All of these theories represent a transmission of desymbolized or deformed images, which cannot cohere for the child and which leave him overwhelmed with death anxiety and suspicion of counterfeit nurturance. In the child's experience, nurturance is dangerous: he flees from it into isolation, stasis, a safer death of his own.

It may require several generations to produce a schizophrenic person. But one can say that, however the inheritance mechanism may operate, whatever the contribution of genetic legacy, the early life of the schizophrenic is flooded with death anxiety, and the result is thought disorder and impairment of reality sense. The schizophrenic's behavior and symptoms represent alternate tendencies of surrender to death anxiety and struggle against it. The near total suspicion of counterfeit nurturance which characterizes the schizophrenic's emotional life renders his psychic numbing more extensive and more enduring than in any other form of psychiatric disturbance. Although one sometimes sees in acute forms of schizophrenia an exaggerated response to stimuli, the general and long-range process is one of profound psychic numbing. To the schizophrenic, as to certain survivors of mass holocausts, life is counterfeit, inner death is predominant, and biological death is unacceptable. Because the schizophrenic's entire existence has been a series of unabsorbable death immersions and survivals, he ultimately settles for a devil's bargain: a lifeless life.

The paradigm of death and continuity of life I have elaborated here—together with psychoformative and psychohistorical perspectives—can help keep psychiatry and psychoanalysis close to their biological origins without imposing on them an instinctual determinism. The paradigm recognizes the scope of man's symbolization and provides a link between his biology and his history, a link that must be made if either is to be sustained.

I close with a few quotations. The first is a slogan from an eighteenth-century guild—very simply, "Remember to die." Ostensibly it was a reminder to make advance funeral arrangements through the guild, but, however inadvertently, it conveys much more. The next is from the playwright Peter Weiss who said, "Once we thought a few hundred corpses would be enough, then we said thousands were still too few; today we can't even count all the corpses everywhere you look." And finally, Yeats:

> Man is in love and loves what vanishes,
> What more is there to say?

REFERENCES

1. Robert Jay Lifton. *Death in Life*. New York: Random House, 1968, 540-41.

2. See Ernst Cassier, *An Essay on Man*, New York: Doubleday Anchor, 1944; *The Myth of State*, New York: Doubleday Anchor, 1946; and *The Philosophy of Symbolic Forms*, New Haven: Yale Univ. Press, 1953-1957; also, Susanne Langer, *Philosophy in a New Key*, Cambridge: Harvard Univ. Press, 1942; *Feeling and Form*, New York: Scribners, 1953; *Philosophical Sketches*, Baltimore: Johns Hopkins Press, 1962; and *Mind: An Essay on Feeling*, Baltimore, Johns Hopkins Press, 1967.

3. Lifton, "Experiments in Advocacy Research," *Research and Relevance*, Vol. XXI of *Science and Psychoanalysis*, ed. J.H. Masserman, 259-71. Also, Newsletter of The American Academy of Psychoanalysis, 16 (1972), 8-13.

4. Thomas Kuhn. *The Structure of Scientific Revolutions*, Chicago: Univ. of Chicago Press, Phoenix Books, 1962.

5. Sigmund Freud. "Thoughts for the Times on War and Death," *Standard Edition*, London: The Hogarth Press and the Institute of Psychoanalysis, 1957, Vol. XIV, 289.

6. Carl Jung. *Modern Man in Search of a Soul*. New York: Harcourt Brace, 1936, 129.

7. Avery Weisman and Thomas Hackett. "Predilection to Death: Death and Dying as a Psychiatric Problem," *Psychosomatic Medicine* 33 (May-June, 1961) No. 3.

8. Otto Rank. *Beyond Psychology*. New York: Dover reprint, 1958, 64.

9. Leslie Farber. "The Therapeutic Despair," *The Ways of the Will*. New York/London: Basic Books, 1966.

10. Marghanita Laski. *Ecstasy: A Study of Some Secular and Religious Experiences*, Bloomington: Indiana Univ. Press, 1961.

11. Marcia Eliade. *Cosmos and History: The Myth of the Eternal Return*. New York: Harper Torchbooks, 1959.

12. Lifton. *Revolutionary Immortality: Mao Tse-tung and the Chinese Revolution*. New York: Random House, 1968, 10.

13. Kenneth Boulding. *The Image,* Ann Arbor: Univ. of Michigan Press. 1956.

14. John Bowlby. *Attachment and Loss.* New York: Basic Books, 1969.

15. Melanie Klein, *et al. Developments in Psychoanalysis.* London: The Hogarth Press, 1952.

16. Kenneth Keniston. *Young Radicals.* New York: Harcourt, Brace & Jovanovich, 1968.

17. Lifton. "Protean Man," *Partisan Review,* 35 (Winter, 1968) 13-27; *History and Human Survival.* New York: Random House, 1970, 311-31; *Archives of General Psychiatry* 24 (1971), 298-304.

18. Erik H. Erikson. *Childhood and Society,* New York: Norton, 1950.

19. Lifton. *Home From the War: Vietnam Veterans, Neither Victims Nor Executioners.* New York: Simon & Schuster, 1973.

20. Joseph D. Teicher. "Combat Fatigue or Death Anxiety Neurosis," *Journal of Nervous and Mental Disease* 117 (1953), 234-42.

21. Abram Kardiner. "Traumatic Neuroses of War," *American Handbook of Psychiatry* I (1959), 246-57.

22. Wilhelm Stekel. *Nervous Anxiety States and Their Treatment* (translated by Rosalie Gabler). New York: Dodd Mead & Co., 1923. Cited in Jacques Choron. *Modern Man and Mortality.* New York: Macmillan, 1964, 131.

23. Rank. *Will Therapy.* New York: Knopf, 1950.

24. Freud. *Civilization and Its Discontents.* Standard Edition, Vol.XXI,89.

25. Lifton. *The Broken Connection* (unpublished manuscript).

26. George R. Crupp and Bernard Kligfeld. "The Bereavement Reaction: A Cross Cultural Evaluation," *Journal of Religion and Health* I (1962), 222-46.

27. Freud. "Analysis of a Phobia in a Five-Year-Old Boy," Standard Edition, Vol.X, 5-149.

28. Harold Searles. "Schizophrenia and the Inevitability of Death," *Psychiatric Quarterly* 35 (1961), 631-35.

29. R. D. Laing. *The Divided Self.* Baltimore: Penguin (Pelican), 1965, 176.

30. Primo Levi. *Survival In Auschwitz.* New York: Collier, 1961, 82.

31. See, for instance, various papers in Don B. Jackson (ed.), *The Etiology of Schizophrenia.* New York: Basic Books, 1960.

32. *Ibid.*

IV

The Anticulture of Suicide

BENJAMIN B. WOLMAN

ONE OF THE MEMBERS OF THE RODENT FAMILY, THE NORWEGIAN lemmings, lives in Norway, Sweden, and in the northern part of Russia and Finland. The lemmings are members of the hamster family. They are about five inches long, have short legs and tails, and are covered with a fur coat. They appear in these areas in very large numbers and in cycles of three to four years. Before the onset of their population explosion, there are a few of them around, and they act in a rather shy and cowardly manner. In the second and third years of the cycle, their reproduction rapidly increases. Each female can produce five to eight young lemmings to a litter, and one couple of lemmings can produce up to 16,000 offspring within the cycle of four years.

The behavior of lemmings changes with the rapid growth of their population. They become aggressive, seeking food frantically. They destroy crops, block roads and avenues, and lay waste to whatever they find in their way. They move across the country though hills and meadows, eat whatever they find, and rush toward lakes, rivers, and seas. Within a short time they die out, giving rise to the belief of suicidal mass drowning. Most probably, however, thousands of them become poisoned by some chemical substance produced in their own bloodstream. This substance may make one believe in their intentional mass suicide, but more likely this apparently suicidal process is inherent in the way of life of that species.

Not unlike the lemming, man too seems to be rushing toward his own destruction. In man's case, however, there appears to be more of conscious effort.

When the anthropologist Claude Levi-Strauss was asked what he thought of contemporary humanity, he compared human beings in the 1970's to maggots in a sack of flour. With the increase of the maggot population, maggots become somehow conscious of one another even before they experience any tactile contact, and they secrete toxins which kill at a distance. They poison the flour that they inhabit, and eventually they all die. Something similar, Dr. Strauss said, is happening to humanity in our own time.

THE MEANING OF CULTURE

Culture is the way in which a species lives. The culture of primitive man was one in which hunters and fisherman lived in caves. Our culture is technologica. We build skyscrapers, operate factories, and move around in cars. Culture is the way a species acts in order to survive. The concept of culture includes the behavior of the members of a species, or a group; the ways in which the group acts to secure food, clothing and shelter; and the ways in which a species, clan, or tribe relate to one another in their struggle for survival are intrinsic elements of their culture.

No human being can survive if left totally alone; yet human beings are endowed with a good deal of hostility toward each other. The individual desire for survival, to remain alive with or without others, is deeply embedded in human nature and repeatedly reconditioned and reinforced. Human belligerence, whether it is offensive or defensive, is one of the outstanding psychological elements of the human personality.

One may hypothesize that the origin of human society was *bellum omnium contra omnes*, "the war of all against all"; but the origin of human civilization was certainly related to some sort of spoken or unspoken social agreement (*contrat social*). Human beings have been born with the ability (or have had to learn) to live with one another, for this was the only way that human beings could survive. The Russian social scientist and theoretician of the peaceful branch of anarchism, Peter Kropotkin, dealt with this problem in his book on *Mutual Aid* (1902). Kropotkin subscribed to Darwin's theory of the fight for survival, but brought significant support to the hypothesis that the best way to fight for survival is through cooperation and mutual aid. He described a great many examples taken from animal life and human history which proved that the species which cooperated in the struggle for survival had a better chance to survive than those plagued by inner strife.

While human beings have cooperated with one another to a greater extent than most other species, they also have had more intraspecies fights than any other species. Intraspecies strife and killings are typical of only a few species, such as rats and certain kinds of fish, but they are frequent among human beings. Human history, as described in the mythology of the Israelites and Romans, started with fratricidal acts; Cain killed Abel, and Romulus killed Remus. (This peculiar phenomenon of fratricide requires more attention, and will be analyzed later in this essay.) The way most human groups interacted, however, was not fratricidally but cooperatively. Quite early in human civilization, human groups established laws forbidding fratricidal wars and murder. The early codes of Hammurabi included punishment for murder, and the Ten Commandments stated, with utmost clarity, "Thou shalt not kill." The ancient laws of the Greeks and Romans also insisted on peace, and forbade fratricidal murder. Even in intercity strifes, they imposed restraint and periods of compulsory peace.

Civilization started with these restraints. I have defined culture (I am using the terms culture and civilization interchangeably) as a *way of life directed towards the protection of life;* the life of the individual and of the group, society, and/or species. Were the purpose of life not to live, there would be no room for anything else, because death is a given that comes whether one asks for it or not.

The question that human beings have faced from the inception of humanity on earth was how to stay alive. Human beings have invented whole sets of procedures, mechanisms, and devices to protect life. The totality of these devices is called culture.

THE MEANING OF FREEDOM

When Hitler started his wars against the Jews, Poles, French, and the British, he wanted only one thing: freedom for himself and slavery for others. He struggled for his own *Lebensraum*, assuming that there was not enough room for the Germans in Germany. The Germans had to spread around the world like lemmings and destroy everything in their way.

Today, Germany has absorbed millions of Germans from territories occupied by the Russians and the Poles, and also invited three million foreign workers. With all of this (imaginary) overpopulation. Germany is a blossoming country and has a most prosperous economy, while in Hitler's time, with much less of a population, Germany was hungry for new conquests and new territory.

Social bonds are based on a restraint of the freedom of individuals. Were each individual free to do what he wished, his social group would plunge into continuous war of all against all. Were each individual free to act upon his desires and needs, he would take away from other individuals the possibility of survival. Since the human species is particularly belligerent, and its levels of self-control and inhibitions are not particularly high, a society that permitted complete freedom for all its members would end in mass murder, which is tantamount to mass sucide. Thus, all societies practice some degree of restraint, for such restraint is necessary for their survival (4).

Moral behavior always involves relationships with other individuals. Morality has but one source, which is the desire to stay alive. Out of practical considerations, people have concluded that one cannot survive in an environment where everyone is free to do as he pleases. Morality leads to a restraint of one's freedom, and allows the same amount of freedom to all. On the primitive level, this restraint is imposed from without, by a physical, political, or symbolic authority in the form of religious commandments sent by God. This is the essence of the moral teachings of all religions. In Judaism and Christianity, for example, the idea of "service to God" is linked with "service to humanity." Religions symbolize the wisdom of generations, based on the fact that a society torn by inner strife has less chance for survival than a society comprised of individuals who cooperate with and support one another.

The question as to how societies cooperate can be answered by looking at those that produce goods necessary for everyone. Even primitive societies practice some degree of division of labor. Division of labor, as described by the sociologist, Emile Durkheim, is the fundamental rule common to practically all social orders. People produce various goods, but these goods are not used exclusively by the producers themselves. A shoemaker, for example, produces shoes which are needed not only by himself, but by a great many people. The more complex the fabric of social relations and the higher the technological development, the more intricate is the division of labor and the ensuing economic interdependence. Absolute freedom for individuals is thus incompatible with technological development. The higher the level of economic development, the more urgent is the need for voluntary self-restraint.

Even primitive societies practice cooperation in hunting and fishing, in agriculture and industry, in peace and in war. All societies impose some sort of peaceful co-existence between its members by erecting a system of justice and by policing. All societies impose laws, and though some laws may be more just than others, all legal systems respresent a certain minimum morality, in the sense of consideration for one's fellow man and recognition of his rights.

Legal systems can be more or less democratic, and more or less concerned with the well-being of all; but no society can tolerate complete chaos and freedom for all.

From Perspiration to Aspiration

In order to satisy their basic needs, people have worked and perspired. With the development of technology, the number of hours one spends at work has been greatly reduced. The reduced workload has its benefits, but also creates problems. With the reduction of the necessary amounts of work, with the general increase of economic well-being and a higher level of gratification of fundamental needs, the amount of necessary perspiration has been substantially reduced.

Certainly, no society can survive unless it produces food, shelter, clothing, and so on. As more people move away from this process, fewer people are needed to produce food necessary for the society. In agricultural societies, almost 100 per cent of the population tilled the soil. Today, 10 to 20 per cent of the population can produce enough food for the entire population. With this gradual shift from perspiration to aspiration, human life becomes more enriched. More people are involved in the arts and sciences, and are devoted to noneconomic professions. More people can produce music instead of producing shoes, or paint canvases instead of walls.

The progress of culture, however, also has its dark side. Many people do not actively participate in the process of perspiration, nor do they enter the process of aspiration. These are the opulent people, the parasitic class, the jet set who possess a good deal of economic power without using it productively. Unfortunately, this class of wealthy and idle people exercises a tremendous influence on the rest of society. Having nothing to gain and so much to lose, they display their arrogance in every possible way. Newspapers and other mass media describe their extravagant lives. Magazines are full of pictures of people who marry and divorce, bear children and then reject them, who waste money in nonsensical ways, yawning away their days and spreading their anticultural poison. Some people in the past lived this way—kings and courtesans; perverted monks and adventurous princesses; but their lives were private and their impact upon the masses rather limited. Today, with mass communications, and in this country especially, with its general admiration of money and widespread conspicuous consumption, these individuals exercise a considerable influence on youth, poor and rich alike.

In an atmosphere of emptiness, in a climate in which nothing amounts to anything, bored and disappointed individuals often resort to violence. Violence in our society is most often combined with robbery and rape. Indeed, materialistic and pragmatic culture has created a particular type of anticultural violence—it is practiced most often for practical gain.

Practical violence is not, however, an absolutely general phenomenon. Some radical groups preach impractical revolutionary ideals, refusing to recognize that they do not have a chance of producing any significant social change through violence. The only thing they elicit is counter-violence. The tragic events on many college campuses in the last few years are a case in point. Violence breeds violence, and whoever uses violence must be aware of the fact that his violence will be counteracted with someone else's violence. When one destroys an office of a university, he doesn't effect any significant change in the structure of American society. The growing tendency to use force, however, does bear witness to the decline of interpersonal cooperation, and consideration of one individual for another. And the decline of cooperation and consideration, the fundamental rules of any culture, is ominous.

HISTORICAL LESSON

We are not the first society to experience this process of anticulture. Similar processes took place in ancient Rome. The level of perspiration declined as the Roman Empire came to receive more and more of its goods from its provinces. Many of the Romans had no need to work, and even more people could find no work.

Their great capital city was divided between the luxurious mansions of Palatium and the slum shacks of Insulae. Some individuals wined and dined day and night at no expense to themselves, while in the same city tens of thousands lived on public welfare. Slum houses were fire traps, and so when Nero set fire to the Insulae, he burned people alive.

Entertainment was available to everyone, and the poor joined the rich in watching brutal fights in which specially trained slaves murdered one another. The Roman Circus had a stage on which people were thrown to wild beasts. When the slaves were killed, the Roman mob experienced great satisfaction and pleasure, not unlike the vicarious pleasure we can experience today by watching crime and murder on television.

It is indeed difficult to be optimistic about the progress of humanity. There are too many similarities between Petronius's Satyricon and what is occurring right now. Sexual orgies, a decline of family ties, the spread of homosexuality—which in terms of the survival of the species is a suicidal phenomenon—a lack of goals and ideals, and senseless efforts to get as much food and sex as possible. All these things link the Roman euphoria in its last days to our own times. *Carpe diem*—"Enjoy the day"—was a slogan of the Roman rich, and is also the motto of our contemporary jet set.

In times that lack a sense of purpose, the only thing to do is to do something for kicks. Thus, our times have brought a widespread wave of violence and terror: Arabs against Israelis, gangs against gangs in America, Catholics against Protestants in Ireland, and so on and so on. All these acts of terror are patently absurd, because no one has ever won anything in this manner and the terrorist groups cause most harm to themselves.

Terror has always produced more terror; thus, from the point of view of society at large, terror has always been an act of suicide. It is significant that most individuals who practice terror, whether in the past or in the present, have been willing to die together with their victims. The terrorists risk their own lives as if their lives have no more meaning to them than the lives of their victims. The currently widespread wave of terrorism is thus a wave of homicide combined with suicide.

DISINHIBITION

Strangely enough, this suicidal wave of anticulture has also influenced the treatment of mental disorders. Mental disorders are caused partially by organic and partially by environmental factors, especially by the interaction between the child and his parents. Freud noticed that many emotional problems of his time were created by a too restrictive parental authority and too prudish social climate. He rebelled against this exaggerated restrictiveness, and developed a system of psychotherapy in which the therapist helps the patient to remove infantile inhibitions and evolve more mature and rational adult inhibitions. This was seventy years ago. In today's climate of freedom bordering on licence and decline of parental authority, there is little left of the Victorian *Zeitgeist.* Psychiatrists and psychologists who advocate the removal of a too-restrictive system storm an open door, and when they do so, they close other, very useful doors. To be normal does not mean to be disinhibited. To be normal does not mean to be "natural." The way we live—that is, our culture—is also our nature. It is perfectly "natural" to press the gas pedal down as far as one likes, but this kind of "natural" behavior can kill a great many people, including the driver himself. The only people who enjoy absolute freedom are the completely disinhibited, severe psychotics in the back wards of mental hospitals. All of us who live with other people must practice some degree of inhibition and self-restraint; otherwise we wouldn't be able to live in a society, nor could anyone live with us.

A great many psychologists and psychiatrists, along with some poorly-trained self-appointed group therapists, advocate disinhibition, as if it were the panacea for all mental ills. They seem to assume that the only problem that mentally disturbed people have is that they cannot act spontaneiously, and that if they could follow their impulses, such behavior could restore their mental health. Very early in his work Freud realized that acting out leads nowhere. Psychoanalysis does not remove inhibitions, it enables one to overcome morbid infantile inhibitions and to develop the normal, rational inhibitions of adulthood. Some recent techniques which promote disinhibition, such as touching, acting out, unrestricted sexual behavior, and uncontrollable emotional outbursts foster many forms of psychosis. They may counteract the exaggerated Victorian neurotic self-restraint, but they encourage psychopathic behavior.

The fact that some people in the healing professions have fallen prey to the current of disinhibition and deculturation is perhaps one of the saddest aspects of our *Zeitgeist*. A therapy based on total disinhibition and acting out is part and parcel of this process of deculturation. As more people follow the path of going back to nature and acting out their impulses, the frequency of violent acts will contribute to our suicidal anticulture.

CLINICAL OBSERVATIONS

In over thirty years of clinical practice I have often come across suicidal patients. Fortunately, none of my patients has ever commited suicide, but in seeking ways to keep them from it, I have gained insight into the mechanics of suicidal wishes and attempts.

I have divided all mental disorders into three large categories or clinical types (9), based on the economic aspects of psychoanalytic theory. How much libido or destrudo is invested in oneself or into others seems to me to be one of the most important indicators of the type of clinical disorder. When the entire, or almost the entire, libido is self-cathected in secondary narcissism, the disorders are psychopathic, and can be categorized as narcissistic hyperinstru- mental. The psychopaths are exceedingly selfish. They do not care about others; they cry only when they feel sorry for themselves.

Sometimes they believe that they love someone, but their "love" is exploitative. Psychopaths usually dislike and distrust people. Most psychopaths are paranoid; they do not believe in anyone's sincerity, for they cannot believe that anyone could be different from themselves. They perceive the world as a jungle in which they, as little animals of prey, have to do whatever they must to get away with murder.

In my entire practice I have never known a psychopath who committed suicide or who seriously tried to commit suicide, though one has often threatened suicide in an effort to extort sympathy, compassion, or concessions from others. Psychopaths are not able to love anyone as much as they are able to hate. They do not believe that anyone can love them, and they are rarely disappointed. They are disappointed only when their victims refuse to be exploited. A psychopath may have regrets, but only when his exploitative actions are discovered and frustrated. A psychopath may feel rejected and feel sorry for himself, but he will never commit suicide.

Manic-depressive patients, on the other hand, are prone to suicide. They think of suicide when they feel rejected and unloved.When they believe that nobody cares for them, their lives seem not worth living. The most dangerous hours for suicidal attempts by manic-depressives are the early morning hours, when their family and friends are asleep. Manic-depressive psychotics fall asleep easily, but they tend to wake up early. Quite often, when they are lying awake in the wee hours and there is no one around to show them how much he loves them, they desire to punish themselves and those whom they feel do not love them. Manic-depressive patients hate those who do not love them; they hope that their suicide will evoke sorrow in those they wanted to love. Some manic-depressive patients have fantasies about lying in caskets and seeing their mothers and fathers, lovers and spouses, crying and regretting the fact that they did not love them.

Manic-depressive patients suffer from what I have called *dysmutual* disorders. *Dysmutual* means being unable to relate to people on a rational, mutual level. The dysmutuals are, as Freud said, love addicts, and rarely if ever can anyone meet their exaggerated demands. Feeling unloved, they experience depressive moods. Depression is basically a self-directed aggression; the dysmutuals hate themselves because no one loves them, and they therefore hate whoever does not love them.

The third category, the *hypervectorial* patients, encompasses all types and degrees of schizophrenia. *Hypervectorial* means that they have directed their lives *away from themselves*. They tend to over-invest their emotions in relationships with other people, following their childhood patterns of becoming overinvolved with their parents or parental substitutes (8). Their parents fail to find emotional satisfaction in the relationship with their spouses, and expect the children to compensate for what they had not received in their own childhoods, and what they feel is lacking from their marital partners.

Children brought up in an atmosphere of an overdemanding emotionality feel that their very survival depends on protecting their protectors. They are prematurely forced to become emotional givers. Since no one can give more than he has, preschizophrenic children arrive at a point where there is not enough love left for themselves, so that a slight frustration or disagreement may cause a psychotic breakdown.

Schizophrenics would like to be loved and to give love, but they fear becoming overinvolved and thus vulnerable; therefore they tend to develop symptoms of withdrawal. Quite often they give the impression of being shallow and unemotional, for they fear that as soon as they might become involved, they would be rejected.

I have worked with several schizophrenics, especially of the simple deterioration type, who have often attempted suicide, especially when they felt that the members of their families or friends whom they trusted have betrayed them. The feelings of rejection and betrayal were the worst blows to whatever zest for life they might have had.

A few years ago a young woman was brought to my office by the members of her family. She had tried to commit suicide the night before by swallowing an enormous number of sleeping pills. Fortunately, her attempt was discovered, and she was immediately taken to the hospital where her stomach was pumped. When she finally would talk to me, she said, "I have nothing to live for." Her story was typical of the schizophrenic type of suicide attempt. She had met a young man who tremendously impressed her (schizophrenics are easily impressed by rambunctious, aggressive, psychopathic types). He was married, but he told her he was single, that he loved her, and that he wanted to marry her. After a few months, when she had slept with him and had allegedly become engaged to him, he admitted that he was already married and had no intention of marrying her.

The fact that he was married hurt her badly. The fact that he broke off with her despite his assurance of great love was an even worse blow. But the most devastating fact was that he had cheated her. She quit her job and broke off all social contacts; she felt that life was not worth living. The loss of faith in someone she loved had made her life worthless, and she decided to put an end to it.

No One Can Be Trusted

The feeling that life is not worth living because no one can be trusted seems to me the crux of the suicidal problem. The maggots poison the flour they live in. The lemmings probably are driven to death by some chemical substance in their bloodstream. The equivalent human poison is the feeling that no one can be trusted.

The human child is born totally unprepared for independent life, and newborn humans will not survive unless they are taken care of. Moreover, as Sullivan, Horney, and Spitz have observed, physical care is not enough, for human infants cannot survive on food alone. Milk is not enough; human beings need love and affection.

Biologically speaking, the human species is made up of billions of creatures who may hallucinate power that they do not possess. No human being is omnipotent and immortal, and even the strongest and smartest individuals will die or be killed. No human being can stand alone and cooperation is a prerequisite for the survival of all individuals. When individuals do not feel accepted, and are unable to trust their friends and allies, they may feel so vulnerable that they give up all hope. Clinical studies corroborate this observation. They hypervectorials (schizophrenics) feel betrayed by their parents, whom they feel they have loved in vain. The dysmutual (manic-depressive) types simply feel rejected. Both clinical types show a high incidence of suicide attempts. But this observation reaches beyond pathology. Contemporary society, with its growing mechanization and alienation, does not contribute much warmth and affection to interindividual relations. Therefore, the chances of suicide are high (2, 3, 5).

INVOLVEMENT AND BETRAYAL

The fact that the hyperinstrumentals (psychopaths) rarely if ever commit suicide, and the dysmutuals (manic-depressives) have a high incidence of suicide sheds additional light on the problem. The hyperinstrumental psychopaths are overinvolved in themselves; their libido is self-hypercathected, and very little, if any, of their emotions are invested in other people. They are self-centered, selfish, and self-loving, and they never develop close human relationships. On the other hand, the dysmutuals desperately need to be accepted. Whenever they feel rejected, their world crumbles and they tend to become suicidal.

These two clinical situations explain certain issues related to the incidence of suicide in modern societies. The psychopaths don't invest anything in others; therefore, they cannot lose anything. Whether their friends and associates love them or don't love them doesn't matter; the hyperinstrumentals have not invested anything in them. They don't believe that anybody can really love them, for they themselves don't love anybody. Therefore, their rate of suicide is exceedingly low. On the other hand, the dysmutuals tend to invest their emotions in others and expect much more in return. Usually, they expect too much, for when they love somebody, they love them so much that they are unable to divest themselves of their love objects. However, by the time they realize that their love objects do not love them, they have already overinvested their emotions, and the frustrated love turns into self-directed, suicidal hatred.

At one time I had a woman patient who was married for twenty-seven years to a man who continuously cheated on her and took advantage of her self-sacrificing, masochistic, dysmutual personality. The woman had occasional fits of depression whenever she felt that her husband did not love her, but she somehow expected that eventually love would prevail. At a certain point, she discovered that her husband had cheated on her all through the marriage, that he had a child with another woman, and that he was spending a good deal of time with her while his wife thought he was on business trips. Upon discovering this my patient became overtly suicidal.

Schizophrenics are also prone to suicide, but only in situations which resemble the loss of a love object. Freud's study of mourning and melancholy describes the feeling of people who have lost someone dear to them, a loss that may be exceedingly painful. When we love somebody, we invest our emotions in that person; and when the beloved person dies, the invested emotions are lost. Therefore, we tend to incorporate the image of the beloved one.

It is much easier to take loss by death than loss by betrayal. The loss by betrayal is more severe, for there is no way to internalize the image of the beloved one. The loss of the love object by rejection and, even worse, betrayal is a loss which can seriously damage self-esteem. Death is beyond human control, but betrayal is committed willfully. I believe that the loss by abandonment, breached faith, or betrayal is the most significant cause of suicide.

In regard to schizophrenics, I have noticed that they tend not to commit suicide as long as they develop paranoid mechanisms. Paranoid defense mechanisms seem to be a protection against suicidal attempts; instead of feeling abandoned and rejected, the paranoid schizophrenic rejects those who reject him and blames them for everything. His destrudo is directed against the outer world, and he blames those who abandoned him. Should this defense mechanism fail, and the paranoid tendencies turn inward and become self-directed, a suicidal attempt may be expected.

Far more frequent are suicide attempts by simple deteriorated schizophrenic patients who feel abandoned. After having invested their emotions in their parents and other significant figures, they arrive at the sad conclusion that all the sacrifice was in vain and no one really cares for them. Thus, they see no reason for continuing the struggle of life.

LIVING AMONG STRANGERS

These clinical observations may be applied to the general population with appropriate modifications. Modern society, with its multiple ways of communication and transportation, has hitherto unknown possibilities for interpersonal contacts. Physical mobility across oceans and continents enables people to meet many more other people than was ever before possible. Telephone, radio, television, newspapers, lectures, compulsory education for children, and adult education courses have immensely increased the amount of communication between people. Office work, huge factories, political and cultural organizations, trade unions and professional groups, cruises and guided tours expose individuals to many more social contacts than ever before in history. So does living in a big metropolis, with its gatherings, and political meetings.

However, social contacts that are superficial and unstable, as most of these are, do not increase one's feelings of security and acceptance. A modern metropolis is a gathering of millions of lonely strangers who do not trust one another and cannot be sure that the gentleman who invites them to have a cup of coffee is not on leave of absence from Sing Sing, or that the woman who cries for help is not inviting them to be mugged or stabbed. We may say, therefore, that our present society creates feelings of loneliness and rejection, and thereby increases the chances of murder and suicide. Human beings are neither maggots nor lemmings; but the concentration of a great many people in a small territory without proper development of meaningful social bonds largely contributes to the anticulture of suicide.

Huge schools and colleges where thousands of people mill around meeting each other without meeting anyone, seeing thousands of people without recognizing a single face in the crowd—such a society of strangers is conducive to violence directed against others and against oneself. One does not kill a friend, but one may have less inhibition when facing strangers. One does not kill oneself when one feels accepted and secure, but when one's social bonds are meaningless, and one realizes that no one cares, and there is no one to be trusted, one may turn hostile feelings loose against oneself and/or whoever is the true or imaginary cause of disenchantment.

Anyone who walks in the mountains of Switzerland can be sure that every passerby will greet him. People do not fear that someone might hurt them. They help others, and they do not feel that strangers intend to grab their money, or hurt them. Their way of life is a civilized society, with small groups, friendly human relationships, and a tradition of personal contact. Nothing like Swiss behavior can be expected in New York or Detroit. There, huge groups of people create a poison like the poison produced by maggots. The estrangement inherent in our way of life; the decline of family ties; the depersonalization in human relations; and the loss of the individual in a mass society are probably the main, or at least the important, reasons why so many people now tend to hurt one another and to hurt themselves.

REFERENCES

1. Berkowitz, L. (Ed.) *Roots of Aggression.* New York: Atherton, 1969.

2. Durkheim, E. *Suicide.* Glencoe, Ill.: Free Press, 1951.

3. Farber, M. *Theory of Suicide.* New York: Funk & Wagnalls, 1968.

4. Freud, S. *Civilization and its Discontents,* Standard Edition, Vol.21. London: Hogarth, 1961.

5. Henry, A.F., and Short, J.F. *Suicide and Homicide.* Glencoe, Ill.: Free Press, 1954.

6. Kropotkin, P. *Mutal Aid.* London: Allen & Unwin, 1902.

7. Meerloo, J.A. *Suicide and Mass Suicide.* New York: Grune & Stratton, 1962.

8. Wolman, B.B. *Children Without Childhood.* New York: Grune & Stratton, 1970,

9. Wolman, B.B. *Call No Man Normal.* New York: International Universities Press, 1973.

10. Wolman B.B. "Success and Failure in Group Psychotherapy," *Proceedings Kingress fur Gruppentherapie,* 1974.

V

My Own Suicide

I AM STILL VERY MUCH ALIVE, ENJOYING LIFE, AND HOPING IT WILL continue for many years to come. Why then contemplate my own suicide?

For one thing, like all forms of death, suicide is a reality. It happens. It happens in all times and in all places. And, like other dimensions of reality, it lends itself to scrutiny. One can pretend it isn't there and ignore it, but it happens nonetheless.

For another, although I myself have never once seriously entertained such a notion, I have known people who have killed themselves. I know others who say they might. As a psychoanalyst, I am not infrequently contacted by persons close to the act. These realities subject me to the profoundest of moral dilemmas, and have triggered deeply moving emotional experiences.

I long ago surrendered the arrogance of believing that I am better than persons less fortunate than me, finally realizing that to condemn them for their misfortune is simply to flatter myself for my own lucky circumstances. We are all so much more fragile than we know, and our strength can dissolve into weakness with a turn of the wheel of fortune. Not because we are simply will-less motes swept along by the winds of fate; but rather because what we feel and do can hardly be understood apart from our past and present life circumstances. Banality though it may be, we must all bear in mind that, "There but for the grace of God go I."

For these reasons, I feel impelled to investigate my own attitudes, values, and beliefs about suicide, and to contemplate what circumstances, if any, could possibly lead me to that final precipice. What follows here, then, is simply a personal statement about how I might feel and behave if I were faced by a suicide of an acquaintance, intimate friend, patient, loved one, or myself.

For the living, death can be merciful exit that ends all human suffering. The knowledge that I have the option to end my life if suffering becomes more than I wish to bear sometimes makes it possible to continue to live through great adversity. Hence, the option of suicide is a precious one. To be condemned to live under great duress can be a greater punishment than to be condemned to die. To be condemned to live forever in misery is a fate almost too terrible to contemplate. The knowledge that suffering can be ended at will somehow makes it seem less unbearable. It reduces the categorical imperative "I have to live" to "I choose to live."

Contemporary proscriptions respecting suicide revolve largely around moral-religious and psychiatric issues: to attempt to kill oneself is immoral or sick. To do so condemns one to the eternal fires of hell or to the twin horror of a lunatic asylum.

I am personally convinced that under the right life circumstances, I would end my own life. It is difficult to anticipate the situations that would provoke me to do this, but were I of advanced age, enduring great physical pain and debilitation, and facing the certainty (or at least the reasonable certainty) of impending death, I would prefer to be put out of my misery rather than to eke out a few more weeks or months of painful consciousness.

It is true we never know the future and that rescue or cure may be just around the corner. The argument is, therefore, that we should hold out until the end. But living life always entails making decisions about the future, with no ultimate guarantees that the decisions are right. Boarding a jet plane puts one's life in jeopardy; but one weighs the risks and the probabilities, and then makes a choice. Few terminal cancer victims so far, had they elected to die before allowing the disease to run its course, could have been blamed for not waiting to find out what might have happened. To elect death is a grave decision, to be sure, and one is wise to weigh all of the contingencies before taking the leap. But as far as the commandment, "Thou shalt not kill" is concerned, I take it to mean that "Thou shalt not kill others."

My willingness to consider ending my own life hinges upon two of my elemental and unprovable beliefs. The first is my moral and philosophical commitment to the proposition that people are the caretakers of their own lives, and have an absolute right to surrender them. The second pertains to my conception of death. Were these beliefs to turn out to be false (and I concede that they might), all of my arguments would collapse. The first belief is a value judgment, subject to change by sufficiently persuasive arguments; the latter is a fact, subject to change by new evidence.

The paradox in my thinking and behavior consists of my reluctance, or at least my difficulty, to freely allow others to have the same freedom of choice which I so jealously reserve for myself. Although suicide seems to me to be everyone's fundamental right, my willingness to let others exercise this right seems somehow to be limited by their closeness to me. I feel much more detached about the suicides of strangers than I do about persons I love or who are my patients. Although this attitude seems obvious and natural enough, a careful analysis of the reasons for it reveals what I believe to be the crux of the problems surrounding the suicide question.

To contemplate one's death is not an easy thing to do, for terror of something beyond the grave "gives us pause," as Hamlet says. Of course, what happens after death is unknown, perhaps unknowable. But our beliefs about it are not; and to a large extent, beliefs determine our actions while we are yet alive. What a person believes will determine whether he embraces or opposes dying. To thwart another's decison to die is therefore to value my own beliefs above his.

My own attitude toward suicide derives naturally from the convictions I hold about life and death. The life to which I am referring is not biological life, although that is certainly involved, but experiential existence—consciousness. In Ronald Laing's sense, I am concerned with the death of the person, not the organism, the mind, not the body.

So-called natural death occurs when biological death renders the continued survival of the mind an impossibility. In suicide, the process is reversed. The mind elects to destroy the body in order to destroy itself. If it were possible to destroy consciousness forever while keeping the biological organism alive, the intentions of most suicides would effectively be accomplished.

Death comes only to the living. Although biological life processes occur before birth, even before conception— consider Weissman's notion about the mortality of the soma and the immortality of the germ plasm—experiential life and the appearance of consciousness occur later. The point is that death, whether defined in experiential or biological terms, is not a state of being or a process, but an absence of life. To experience death, one has to be alive. The dead thing is recognized as dead precisely because it is incapable of consciousness or of experience. Therefore, death has meaning only to cogniscient persons.

If death does refer to the nonexistence of life, a number of interesting corollaries follow. For one thing, we can experience or at least contemplate our own state of nonexistence as we nonexperienced it before we were born, much as in waking we can experience our own absence of consciousness during sleep. But is it believable or at all probable that, unborn, we can experience or contemplate our own existence in life? I think not. The condition of being dead mirrors the condition of being unborn. One can contemplate the state of nonexistence in death by virtue of the fact that we can contemplate our own previous state of nonexistence. I am not prepared to defend the propositions that we have had no previous lives, or that there is no life after death, though indeed this is what I believe. I am merely addressing myself to the problem of how to conceptualize the condition of being dead as a state of nonexistence, especially since so many existing persons find it difficult to conceptualize or to understand nonbeing.

What then is the view from the grave? There is none. How one lives life has meaning only to the living. Meanings come into being and disappear with life itself. To the dead, the question of how they lived their lives, whether for better or worse, in sickness or in health, good, bad, or indifferent, is meaningless. From the point of view of the dead person himself, it is meaningless to ask whether his suicide was justified or not. This question has meaning to a person only so long as he is alive.

One can therefore examine the justification or legitimacy of a suicide only from the point of view of the living, whether the living be the person himself or others connected with him. Since the person who succeeds at suicide ceases to exist, the only persons upon whom his suicide can possibly have an impact (in existential and experiential terms) are those who survive and have been in contact with him. It is to them that the suicide has meaning. Our analysis of suicide must thus be shifted from an examination of the dead to analysis of the living. The paradox in my thinking about suicide—the difficulty I have in allowing others I am involved with to freely commit suicide—means that I do not want them to kill themselves because of the effect of their suicide upon me!

The thought of my own death may sadden me and change the quality of my experience, or it may gladden me. I am not the first to have noted the quasi-euphoria that appears in a suicidal depressive once he has arrived at the decision to end his existence. The thought about others dying may also sadden or gladden me in proportion as I love and need them or hate them. Obviously I do not want to lose persons whom I need or who are important to me.

Most persons are embedded in a social network of other persons who would be affected by their deaths. My suicide affects others, theirs affect me. Much of the concern about suicide in both personal and professional terms reflects this interdependence. However much I may argue that interposing myself between a person and his wish to die is in the service of "helping" him, to a greater or lesser extent I am usually also serving my own values and self-interests, even in those instances in which the victim himself is grateful to me for my intervention.

Self-examination of my efforts to prevent patients from suiciding inevitably confronts me with motives for doing so that I have the greatest difficulty in acknowledging; my narcissism, my guilt, my professional reputation, my rage, my omnipotence, and my fear. These same base motives—in addition to selfishness and need—also are at the root of how I react to the threat of the loss of loved ones, since it is I, not they, who must suffer the consequences of their death. I can hardly communicate the full flavor of the satisfaction and joy I feel knowing that, after two unsuccessful suicide attempts and a commitment to a mental hospital, a youthful patient of mine now lives happily in California. Nor can I express my shock and remorse when I learned that a patient of mine had ended his life, even though I knew that he had been miserable for many years.

Death wears many faces, of course; and we identify a death as a suicide only when we believe that the victim has exercised some control over the means by which he died. This assignment of responsibility makes the response to a suicidal act different from the response to any other of the ways in which people lose their lives.

Persons who die through other means than suicide rarely earn opprobrium. We sympathize with the victims of lethal disease, and with those who die through events over which they have no control; we do not blame them for dying. There is one exception to this—patients who report being angry at their parents for having died when they were still children. These people blame their dead parents for having abandoned them, and construe their deaths as a hostile or at least an unloving and selfish parental act. But suicides are different in this respect—often their deaths are viewed as somehow shameful.

There are those of us who allow other individuals to assume full responsibility for their own lives, insofar as they do not intrude upon the lives of others. There are those of us who arrogate to ourselves the responsibility for the lives of others. The ultimate philosophical merits of these opposed positions will not be argued here. But it is clear that our attitudes toward a threatened suicide, or to an accomplished one, will very much reflect whether we assign the responsibility for the outcome to ourselves, or to the other. It is perhaps not merely coincidental that suicidal persons often endeavor to assign responsibility for themselves to others.

The death of any of us affects the lives of all of us. Sometimes these effects go unnoticed, but at other times they are overwhelming. The loss of a parent is a monumental event in the life of a child. The loss of a spouse can be equally crushing. How much more devastating, then, are the effects of the death by suicide of a person with whom we are intimately involved! For, besides the awful feeling of loss that the death engenders, we may have to confront terrible feelings of guilt which are directly related to our sense of responsibility.

My posture with respect to my own or another's suicide is thus inextricably connected to my ownership of responsibility for my own life, or for theirs. If I accept full responsibility for my life, I demand full responsibility for my death. If I accept and am allowed full responsibility for my own life, then nobody else need feel responsible for me if I determine to die. But if I accept or assume responsibility for the lives of others, then it is I, not they, who decide whether their death is allowable.

If I truly care for others, in the sense so ably elucidated by Milton Myeroff, I experience them as an extension of myself, and at the same time as something separate from me that I respect in its own right. If I care for others, then of course I consider the effect of my death upon their lives. To the extent that I feel responsible for them, I may renounce my own needs in favor of theirs. In like manner, if I care for another, I will weight the effects of their death upon me; and to the extent that I am able to take responsibility for myself, I may be able to renounce my own needs in favor of theirs. This means assuming full responsibility for the effects upon me of their decision to die. In so doing, I free them of responsibility for me and enable them to do what their heart dictates.

In the end, it is my caring, in a responsbile way, that permits me to separate love from self-interest, and to surrender my life or to accept the suffering I must endure in allowing another to meet his destiny.

If I truly care for someone, I can let go.

VI

Personal Situation as a Factor in Suicide, with Reference to Yasunari Kawabata and Yukio Mishima

MAMORU IGA

SUICIDE HAS BEEN EXTENSIVELY STUDIED FROM PSYCHOLOGICAL or social-structural points of view. However, what determines a behavior is the emotional meaning which a personality in a particular psychological condition gives to the immediate environmental situation. The emotional meaning is a product of interaction between personality and physical-social-cultural environments. Therefore, the primary contribution of sociological studies of suicide may be considered to be the clarification of a series of fields in which suicidogenic interaction takes place. The series of the fields may be called a personal situation. The distinction between personal and environmental situations seems to be important, because most sociologists, with few exceptions, (1) focus their analyses almost exclusively upon the environmental situation.

The criticism applies to a certain extent to Durkheim, too, whose study of suicide has been a fountainhead of most studies of suicide in sociology, although he was not an environmental determinist. His awareness of the importance of psychological factors is indicated by his key concepts, such as solidarity (attraction of the group to its members, the degree of which distinguishes egoistic from altruistic suicide), and external regulation (felt restraint, the degree of which distinguishes anomic from fatalistic suicide). Both are psychosocial concepts. In addition, his analysis of suicide is strewn with psychological concepts, such as a desire for the meaning of life; unconscious wish for sympathy; depression and melancholoy; mystical joy; the sense of a "future pitilessly blocked and passion violently choked"; a sense of relative deprivation; and so on. (2)

Durkheim's typology of suicide has been criticized as inapplicable to individual suicides, despite the fact that he suggested this possibility in his chapter on "Individual Forms of the Different Types of Suicide" (3). There his types of suicide were described in terms of behavior traits on five levels: cultural system, personality system, social relational system, crisis situation, and psychological condition. The cultural system is represented by self- or collectivity-oriented values, and the personality system by the orientation to institutional means for goal attainment. The social-relational system is divided into relational (as represented by the degree of social restraint), attitudinal (as shown by the degree of self-assertiveness), communicational (degree of communication with social objects), and evaluational traits (criteria for evaluation of received communication). A suicide type is interpreted as a pattern or configuration produced by the combination of traits; a single trait does not necessarily determine a type.

The egoistic suicide is described in the following terms: someone who has self-oriented goals based on a philosophical cultural principle; nonconforming means for goal attainment; weak (or weakly felt) social restraint; a high degree of demand and self-expression; a low degree of received communication; and highly individualistic criteria for evaluating received communications. This type of person may crave some meaning for his life which is obtainable only by social attachment (4). He may suffer a conflict between selfish goals and unconscious wishes for response and recognition. In a frustrating situation, he may have difficulty with meaningful communication, and may lose the courage to live.

The altruistic suicide involves a person who is characterized by a belief that group goals override individual ones; a high degree of conformity; strong social restraint. He sees individual demands and self-expression as subordinate to group goal-attainment; he has a high degree of communication, and follows group criteria for the evaluation of received communication. This type of person may be motivated to kill himself because of a sense of obligation, shame, and guilt. He may even experience mystical joy in suicide, because he regards the death for a group goal as the highest kind of individual goal.

The fatalistic suicide is characterized by a loss of both group and individual goals; a high degree of conformance and dependence; strong social restraint; or strong sensitivity to it. He has a low degree of individual demand and self-expression, a low degree of communication, and follows group criteria in the valuation of received communication. The psychological condition of this type of person is characterized by the feeling that "the future is blocked and passion violently choked," and by resentment, fear, and resignation. These conditions are correlated with an inclination toward the wish to be killed, as manifested by submission, masochism, self-blame, and self-accusation, in addition to a sense of helplessness, fatigue, and despair.

The major features of the anomic suicide are a marked self-profit motive; ambivalence between conformance-dependence and a compulsive wish for autonomy; declining social restraint; a high degree of individualistic demands and self-expression; a declining degree of communication; and inconsistent criteria for the evaluation of received communication. This type of person suffers from a great goal-means discrepance, and a sense of relative deprivation. There is a vicious cycle between the inflated ego ideal and a dependency need, producing unlimited anxiety. The psychological conditions typical of this type are greed, vanity, disillusionment, feverish imagination, and jealousy. Another characteristic is the tendency to be hostile towards others, similar to

Menninger's wish to kill, as represented by accusation, blame, revenge, and arrogance.

In a previous work, these indicators were applied in a somewhat impressionistic way to 68 completed suicides by Kyoto University students, which had occurred during the period from 1953 through 1968. No egoistic suicide was found in comparison with possibly three altruistic, 13 fatalistic, and 52 anomic suicides (5). In this study, the same indices were applied to the suicides of two prominent Japanese writers: Yasunari Kawabata, the Nobel Prize winner for literature in 1968, and Yukio Mishima, a Nobel Prize candidate in the same year.

Kawabata left his home in Kamakura in the afternoon of April 16, 1972, for his workroom in nearby Zushi. There was no sign of suicidal intention. That evening he was found dead with a gas conduit in his mouth in the room, which commanded magnificent views of both ocean and mountains. He was 72 years old. Mishima committed *hara-kiri* on November 25, 1970, with one of his admirers, following the traditional *samurai* ritual. He did so after delivering an impassioned plea to 1,200 members of the Self-Defense Forces from the balcony of its Tokyo headquarters for an uprising to produce a constitutional change to revive the Imperial Army. He was 45 years old.

The application of Durkheim's indices described both suicides as egoistic, although the writers were completely different in personality, philosophy of life, and experiences. Apparently, Durkheim's typology lacks the power to discriminate in individual cases. The primary reason is that it overemphasizes the societal situation at the expense of the personal in a deed in which a personality and the societal situation interact. For Durkheim the overemphasis was probably unavoidable, because he was trying to refute the then-popular psychological reductionistic explanations of suicide by offering an alternative sociological explanation.

Any personal situation is considered to be defined by two aspects: definition of the situation, and adjustive effort. A suicidogenic definition of the situation is produced by the interaction among three factors: (a) wide goal-means discrepancy; (b) the lonely self; and (c) perception of the immediate condition as overwhelming and inescapable. The self-destructive adjustment is composed of:(a) an inadequate coping mechanism;(b) inaccessibility of effective alternative outlets for aggression; (c) a negative view of life, and accepting attitudes toward death and suicide; and (d) a perception of the availability or unavailability of social resources for problem solving. Each of these components is not determined solely by psychology or by society, but by their interaction in the particular situation. The objective of this study is to analyze the personal situations which produced the suicides of Kawabata and Mishima in terms of the components that defined their situations and their adjustive efforts.

GOAL-MEANS DISCREPANCE

Goal-means discrepancy occurs when there is a gap between ego ideal and self-conception. According to Weissman, when successful writers experience the extraordinary gratification of self-esteem, exhibitionism, and omnipotence which accompanies great success, they will establish a new standard to enable them to repeat the past achievement (6). The new goal often produces a gap between their raised ego ideals and self-conceptions based on social responses. Kawabata's deflated self-conception was partly due to his declining physical strength, and partly to the great public popularity which the Nobel Prize brought to him. The popularity was exploited by politicians, and Kawabata, whose whole life had been devoted to aestheticism, suddenly became involved in politics. His involvement was emotional, because of his hostility against progressivism, and produced a psychological disequilibrium (7). Consequently the defeat of Hatano, a conservative candidate for the Mayorality of Tokyo for whom Kawabata had campaigned vigorously, was probably a blow to his ego.

The deflated self-conception seems to be more important in Mishima's suicide, because of his highly narcissistic temperament. According to two popular magazines which published special issues on Mishima shortly after his death (8), 65 per cent of 41 critics attributed his suicide to the discrepancy between his ego ideal and his self-conception; 27 per cent attributed it to the discrepancy between his "ideal society" and the actual one; and 8 per cent considered it a love-pact suicide, based on his homosexuality. His narcissism is indicated in his declaration to students at Waseda University in October, 1968: "Regarding the problem of humanism and egoism, I am not the one who can have sympathy with other people; I am only worried about myself" (9). It is also expressed in his reasons for his anti-Communism: "Frankly, I first thought of action. This is the first. I have felt that ideology, idea, and spirit debilitate when there is no enemy. So I wanted to have an enemy at any cost. I decided to have communism as my enemy" (10). His anti-Communistic stance is almost like a toy for him. His narcissistic obsession about appearances produced a dilemma which he faced on New Year's Day of 1966:

> When I finish this big work [his final tetralogy], I shall be 47 years old, and I shall have to give up forever the opportunity to die a hero's death. Shall I give up a hero's death or shall I complete my life work? (11)

Mishima himself explained his narcissism as a reaction to an inferiority complex acquired during childhood. He was reared by his sickly grandmother, who loved him so much that she took him away from his parents when he was 49 days old. Because of his poor health, she was very indulgent. She reared him as if he were a girl until he was almost 14 years old, when she died. She also reared him in almost complete isolation from his peers, particularly from boys, lest he should learn "bad things" from them; his whole world consisted of picture books and children's stories. Until he was old enough to go to high school, he spoke girls' language. At the Peers' School, which placed a special emphasis on masculinity, he felt ashamed of his girlish language and behavior. He reacted against his frail physique and feminine identification with compulsive masculinity and narcissism. The narcissism was enhanced by his series of easy successes during adolescence and young adulthood; among other awards, he won a silver watch given by the Emperor as the highest honor graduate from the Peers' School. The immediate acclaim that greeted his first novel naturally reinforced and intensified his egotism, as did also the masculine physique he developed by body building. One result was the boastful declaration he made in August, 1970 (12):

> I cannot see any cultural development in post-war Japan of any significance. Poetry? No. Sculpture? No. Theatre? No. In literature, there is only myself.

Given this narcissism, his failure to receive the Nobel Prize must have been a severe blow. In addition, the reaction to his works was not always favorable. Naoya Shiga, generally regarded as the "God of Novels," said once about Mishima: *"Are wa dameda. Yume bakari kaite irukara ikan"* ("He is not good. He writes only dreams.") (13). Hideo Kobayashi, who is often called "God of literary critics" in Japan, remarked that *"Kinkakuji [The Temple of the Golden Pavilion]* is not a novel. It is a lyric produced by Mishima's brain. Despite his superabundant talent, no characters are alive; they give no sense of reality" (14). Mishima's later works were usually regarded by his Japanese colleagues as showing little variation and development (15)—in Shooichi Saeki's opinion, for instance, they showed only "dried-up emotion" (16). Probably, Gore Vidal was right when he said that once Mishima became famous, he was "too quickly satisfied with familiar patterns and did not venture into new patterns of literary art" (17). Seidenstecker, in 1965, pointed out the "intrinsic emptiness" of *Kinkakuji,* suspecting that

Mishima might not have found what he really wanted to write (18); and in 1968, the same critic observed that Mishima seemed to be exhausted. His "recent works have nothing to add to what have been already published in foreign countries. He probably needs to make a new start" (19). Since Mishima continued to be a first-rate critic until his death (20), he must have had extraordinarily high expectations from himself, and surely must have felt diffuse dissatisfaction with the progress of his talent.

Mishima's difficulties, suffered despite his abundant genius, may be explained in terms of his limited life experience. His childhood and adolescence were characterized by the atmosphere of rigidity, fanaticism, indulgence, and detachment from reality, all of which limited his horizons. The resultant boredom and the wish to escape from it are suggested by a poem he composed at the age of 15:

Every evening, I stood by the window
Waiting for some disaster to occur—
For the wicked, ferocious looking dust storm of a calamity
To march in a big wave from beyond the horizon
Like a big dark rainbow.

As a result of his upbringing, Mishima did not know the life of the masses. Even his knowledge of the life of *samurai*, which Mishima romanticized, was limited to the later Tokugawa Period (1600-1867). At that time, the *samurai* was an alienated figure, entirely dependent for his survival upon the rice stipend which his lord bestowed upon him. The cultivation of a spirit of self-sacrifice, which Mishima idealized, was the price for securing the master's protection. The development of a money economy, and a rising standard of living worked hardships on the *samurai*, who relied on rice as their basic income. Their rice had to be changed to its equivalent in money in order to acquire necessities and luxuries, of course, and merchants who rice-brokered and speculated did so at the expense of the *samurai*.

Samurai anxiety due to dependence and economic insecurity was compensated for by prejudice against and maltreatment of commoners. He could even kill them with impunity (21). Consequently, the *samurai* was almost entirely insensitive to the feelings of the majority of his society. The *samurai* culture was an ideal abstraction that disregarded much of humanity as beneath it. Thus, Mishima's idolization of *samurai* symbolized his own detachment from most of human experience, which probably was a handicap for him as a writer. This handicap is evident when we compare Mishima's work with that of Kawabata, or another great Japanese writer, Junichiro Tanizaki, both of whom were well versed in both *kamigata* (Kyoto-Osako) and Tokyo cultures, as well as merchant and *samurai* cultures.

A social goal-means discrepancy, also part of Mishima's life, was the gap between his ideal conception of the world and the actual conditions of post-war Japan. After their defeat in World War II, deprived of their traditional values, especially Emperor worship and militarism, the Japanese people generally turned to a most basic motive—self-interest. Perhaps this was a natural reaction to their traditionally stifled individuality. The self-interest motive was reinforced by the concept of democracy that was imported from Americans. Since American democracy was interpreted only as a claim for individual rights, and Japanese tradition did not prepare people to understand its universalistic aspects (22), the Japanese "democracy" mostly produced men without principle. To this condition, Kawabata and Mishima reacted with intense hostility, because both were staunch believers of what Ben Dasan (23) calls *Nihon-kyo* (Nihonism).

Nihon-kyo is "the strongest religion in the world, because it has been incorporated into the core personality of Japanese people beyond their awareness." Christians, Sooka-Gakkai members, Marxists, or liberals—all generally represent different versions of *Nihon-kyo,* if they are Japanese. *Nihon-kyo,* as a philosophy of life, places primary emphasis on *ninjo*. *Ninjo* sometimes means "humane feelings," in a general sense, but more often it means "sensitivity to the social inferior's dependency need." An example of *ninjo* is that if a person admits his guilt by saying *sumimasen* ("I am sorry"), he should not be punished. *Sumimasen* implies many things: (1) an expression of guilt about the failure to fulfill an obligation to repay a favor (*on*) which the person received; (2) an apology for that failure; (3) an appeal to the superior not to drop him from his favor; and (4) gratitude in advance for continuing favor (24). If a person who says *sumimasen* is punished, the person who punishes must be blamed for having no *ninjo* (25).

The emphasis on *ninjo* is counterbalanced by a stress on *gen-on* ("original obligation") (26), which for Christians is contrasted with *gen-zai* ("original sin"). *Ninjo* shown by a social superior is a favor which its receiver must repay, and which therefore it becomes his obligation to repay—a point of view that has been utilized to stifle dissatisfaction against the superior (27). All Japanese are born obliged to repay favors received from the Emperor (or the nation), parents, teachers, and fellowmen (or society). The ideal society for both Kawabata and Mishima was one based on *ninjo,* with its obligations and familistic relationships.

Related to *ninjo's* particularism and familism is an uncritical attitude toward traditional social structure. Japanese people tend to blame individuals, especially social inferiors, for a social problem, where Americans would tend to blame the social structure as well as responsible individuals (28). When the Japanese do blame their society, they are more likely to blame a non-Japanese element within it than a traditional one. Hence, the confusion of post-war Japan was attributed by both Mishima and Kawabata to American individualism, which they equated with selfishness. Kawabata wanted to return to *furui utsukushii Nihon*—"old beautiful Japan" of the Heian Period (794-1185) (29). Mishima wanted to return to *samurai* Japan before its modernization.

Another element of *Nihon-kyo* is intuitive and mystic

thinking (30). Its followers hold that truth is clear to everybody without verbalization, as indicated by such concepts as *gengai no gen* ("word without wording"), *rigai no ri* ("reason beyond reasoning"), and *hogai no ho* ("law above laws") (31). An outstanding feature of Kawabata's work is his capacity to intuitively grasp and recreate a beautiful image of a fleeting phenomenon (32):

> Outside it was growing dark, and the light had been turned on in the train, transforming the window into a mirror.... In the depths of the mirror the evening landscape moved by, the mirror and the reflected figure like motion pictures superimposed one on the other....The reflection in the mirror was not strong enough to blot out the light outside, nor was the light strong enough to dim the reflection. The light moved across the face, though not to light it up. It was a distant, cold light. *As it sent its small ray through the pupil of the girls's eye, as the eye and the light were superimposed one on the other, the eye became a weirdly beautiful bit of phosphorescence on the sea of evening mountains.*

Mishima's intuitionism is shown by his emphasis on *chikoo gooitsu* (identity of knowledge and action). To him, knowledge was intuitive and experiential; conceptual knowledge was superficial and false.

Kawabata's mysticism is represented by such stories as *Fushi* (*No Death*), in which a couple attempt a double suicide. The girl dies, but the young man fails, and lives to be an old man, suffering from poverty and deafness. After he finally dies, his spirit as an old man returns and unexpectedly meets the spirit of the girl, who is still eighteen years old. Their short conversation is full of calm affection and pathos. Mishima's mysticism is represented by *Eirei no Koe* (*Voice of Dead Heroes*).

In sum, Kawabata and Mishima, who were firm believers in *Nihon-kyo*, championed particularism, familism, traditionalism, intuitionism, and mysticism. Since the materialistic "democracy" in post-war Japan appeared to destroy these ideals, both men reacted with an overwhelming frustration and hostility.

THE LONELY SELF

Kawabata was liked by many people, especially by women, but he could not form really intimate friendships. His loneliness is symbolized by Komako, in *Snow Country,* who "seemed to live alone reading books, without much friendship with fellow villagers" (33). When Fumiko, in *Thousand Cranes,* was asked "Have you been alone since your mother died?" she answers, "Yes. Even with Mother, we lived alone" (34).

The fact that Kawabata was called a *bukimi na hito* (35) "weird person," even by one of his most intimate friends, suggests a lack of genuine intimacy in his associations. His weirdness was primarily due to his detached observant attitude. When Soohachi Yamaoka served with Kawabata as a war correspondent at a Navy *kamikaze* pilot base, he recalls "Every day, without writing for himself, Kawabata gazed from aside rudely at the papers I was working on." The gaze from the expert writer made Yamaoka so uneasy that he begged him not to do it. Kawabata grinned slightly, but he did not stop gazing (36). When a group of dancers visited Kawabata, one of the girls noticed that "*Sensei* (Kawabata) was observing our antics in the same way that he observed fifty birds" (37). His detached attitude is best symbolized by the protagonist, Shimamura, of *Snow Country,* who is transparent and functions only as a mirror for the heroine's psychology. This detachment contributed to Kawabata's greatness as a writer, but it also reflected his lack of intimacy with family members and friends, which probably was one important cause of his suicide.

Kawabata's weirdness and detached attitude are understandable in the light of his childhood experiences. During his first year of life, both his parents died, and he was separated from his only sister, with whom he never had any further contact. The sister died when he was ten years old. When he was seven, his grandmother died, and when he was sixteen, so did his grandfather. With all these deaths, his relationship with his family members was very limited, and his detached attitude was a necessary defense. The loss of his parents at a very early age probably produced a strong sense of deprivation and loneliness, which must have been aggravated by the Japanese idealization of the mother-child relationship. This relationship continues to be very close throughout life, and is the source of stability and strength of families. In such a cultural context, the feeling of having been deprived of maternal love can be tormenting and depressive. One of Kawabata's novels *Nemureru Bijo* (*Sleeping Beauties*), symbolizes a wish to cuddle with and to be warmed by a maternal figure.

Kawabata's sense of deprivation and loneliness must also have been aggravated by Japanese prejudice against orphans. Because Japanese families are so closeknit, people there believe that without parental supervision and discipline, and without economic security, an orphan's personality becomes too warped for him to grow up to be a reliable employee. Thus, good companies, especially banks, do not employ orphans, and people tend to regard them as untrustworthy and inferior. Understandably, such rejection and discrimination make many orphans feel that they are persecuted. The consequent insecurity and paranoiac mistrust may be called the *koji konjo*—"orphan mentality or complex". The orphan complex was a great concern for Kawabata. He wrote, "Desperate from the depressive feeling produced by constant self-examination to see if my personality at the age of 20 had been warped by the *koji konjo,* I started on the trip to Izu" (38). As an orphan, therefore, Kawabata must have experienced a strong sense of deprivation and diffuse loneliness.

Loneliness seems to have played a more important role in Mishima's suicide than in Kawabata's, however, perhaps because of his narcissistic temperament. He had no really intimate friend among his literary colleagues. He felt that "he had been betrayed by his seniors and friends repeatedly" (39). A happy family was an "enemy" to Mishima.(40) This inimical attitude toward others also permeates his view of literature and society. "Since I started as a novelist," he said, "I regard society as my enemy. There can be no writer who is so foolish as to think otherwise" (41).

The mistrust and accompanying loneliness may be explained in terms of Mishima's narcissistic temperament. A core element of narcissism is *amae*—the assumption that others exist to serve one's own needs. Perhaps because of his spoiled childhood, and his easy successes in adolescence and young adulthood, Mishima's *amae* appears to have been close to the infantile sense of omnipotence. Consequently, when his *amae* was not satisfied, the psychological damage would have been unusually severe. This apparently happened at least twice in later life, in addition to his failure to win the Nobel Prize.

In July, 1957, Mishima made a trip to New York for the purpose of arranging for his Noh plays to be performed there; but his expectations were not fulfilled, and on Christmas Eve of that year, when his American friends were celebrating, he disconsolately left the United States for Europe. Donald Keene later recalled that Mishima apparently was dejected by what he must have thought was very "cold" treatment by Americans, including Keene himself (42). The psychological damage which Mishima apparently sustained was expressed in the desperate loneliness of Fujiko in *Kyoko no Ie* (*Kyoko's House*), published in the next year. Fujiko is a daughter of an executive of a big company, of which her husband is an employee. She accompanies her husband to New York, where he is interested in nothing but his own business. In addition, she sees all Japanese there as her "enemies," and her associations with Americans are also not satisfying because she cannot impress them with her wit (43). She becomes desperately lonely:

> Her apartment room, to which she is confined by snow, looks like a prison. Loneliness, burning inside, flushes her

face. Standing up with her cheeks in hands, she walks around in the room. Finally, kneeling down in front of a window, she prays to God, in whom she does not believe: "Please help me! Please save me! I will do anything if you relieve me of this loneliness" (44).

In order to get attention from somebody, she wants to attempt suicide; to break the loneliness, she sleeps with a white neighbor, and hopes that her husband will become angry and punish her (45). Although the degree to which Fujiko's loneliness reflects that of Mishima in New York will never be known, the feeling that he was not treated royally could have hurt his narcissistic ego, since his emotional maturity seems to have lagged far behind his intellectual maturity. The incident may also have helped to change his point of view from aesthetic eroticism to a nationalist didacticism, for next year he wrote the passionately nationalistic *Yuukoku* (*Patriotism*).

The other severe blow to Mishima's ego was that *Kyoko no Ie* (1958), which he thought was a masterpiece, did not meet with acclaim. After this, his work became increasingly more didactic and abstract; and his colleagues generally became increasingly critical of his writing.

Erwin Ringel describes suicide (46) in terms of narrowing perception. Often suicidal persons refuse any offer of assistance; one of the reasons they reject it is that they regard their immediate situation as overwhelming and inescapable. My research of Kyoto University student suicides in 1968 found that impulsivity was highly correlated with suicide. Impulsive persons tend to define their immediate situation as overwhelming and inescapable.

Kawabata's ill health and hostility to the post-war democracy in Japan might have led to the same perception, resulting in despair. He said, "Since the defeat in the last war, I have nothing but to return to *Nihon korai no kanashimi* [the traditional pathos of Japan]. I do not believe in postwar conditions, nor do I believe in reality" (47). Shortly before he received the Nobel Prize, he felt that his body was "crumbling all over" and he was "almost giving up" (48). Mishima expressed a similar feeling in 1965, five years before his death. He was disgusted with literature; he suffered from feelings of helplessness, and thought that nothing he attempted was useful (49). In March, 1970, Mishima said, "Life is a nosedive to decay without any alternative potential left," and he said he wanted to die quickly (50). Just about a week before his death, he said, "I am exhausted...I am disgusted....There is no way out" (51).

How well someone copes is related to his perception of the immediate situation as overwhelming and inescapable. The coping mechanisms which Kawabata and Mishima used can only be inferred from their behavior. Mishima's narcissism apparently was related to weak ego control—that is, he was ineffective in coping with a frustrating situation. The characteristics of narcissism— "vanity; conceit; craving for prestige and admiration; a desire for being loved in connection with an incapacity to love others; withdrawal from others; and anxious concern about health, appearance, intellectual faculties" (52) produce a strong dependency need—that is, a narcissist's security is dependent upon other people's responses. His need interacts with his wish for self-inflation, which in turn impairs his human relations, and ultimately makes for increasingly less effective ways to cope with the world.

The growing ineffectiveness of Kawabata's coping mechanism was indicated by his unusually emotional expression of hostility against "progressive" Mayor Minobe (53), who was generally regarded favorably by Japanese intellectuals, probably including most of Kawabata's friends and colleagues. Seidensticker remembers that Kawabata had never expressed his anger against anybody that emotionally before (54). The decline of his self-control may have stemmed from two sources. One was his habit of taking sleeping pills. Kawabata often suffered from insomnia, and took sleeping pills to ease his tension, frequently to the point where he was found in a daze (55). The other is the impetuosity which may accompany a great success. A great success, such as the Nobel Prize, tends to produce and promote narcissism and a sense of omnipotence (56). The stronger the sense of omnipotence, the less tolerant a person may become. Minobe's popularity among Japanese intellectuals may have irked Kawabata, because Minobe's political progressivism was exactly opposite to his own ideal society, which was that of ancient Japan; and unconsciously, he may have identified himself with the demigods of those ancient days.

ALTERNATIVE OUTLETS FOR AGGRESSION

Suicide is a form of aggression against oneself; consequently, the availability of alternative outlets for aggression is an important factor in whether or not suicide actually occurs. The Japanese show three main patterns of behavior for ego defense: *gruupu maibotsu shugi* (identification with the group); *dentoo maibotsu shugi* (merging oneself in tradition); and *koodo maibotsu shugi* (forgetting frustration by becoming absorbed in compulsive activities) (57). Mishima's behavior may be explained in terms of *dento* and *koodo maibotsu shugi,* as indicated by his glorification of *samurai* tradition and his belief in *chikoo gooitsu* (identity of knowlege and action). However, ultimately all these activities proved ineffective in satisying his narcissistic ego.

Kawabata was an individualist; he called himself *burai no to* (villain), meaning nonconformer. He was a nihilist (58). Therefore, group identification could not help him reduce his tension. Neither could traditionalism. Tradition merely supplied him material for self-expression. Perhaps activities like his writing, making trips to enjoy natural beauty or meeting many people helped to make life bearable; but his involvement in politics, and his declining physical strength, in combination with his old age, deprived him of these pleasures.

ATTITUDE TOWARD LIFE, DEATH, AND SUICIDE

When a person defines his situation as suicidogenic, whether or not he will actually kill himself is mostly determined by his attitudes toward life, death, and suicide. Since both Kawabata and Mishima were *Nihon-kyo* believers, their philosophy of life was basically determined by its fundamental tenets: that our life and death are determined by *tenri* (natural law); that since our life came from eternal Nature, we should be ready to return it there; and that to live according to Nature is to die according to Nature (59). What makes this doctrine uniquely Japanese is the equation of Nature with tradition, so that when their tradition is threatened, Japanese should resist, attack the source of the threat, or even sacrifice themselves to fight it. Thus, both Mishima and Kawabata perceived the significance of life to be primarily merged with tradition, and both accepted death as natural. Beyond these basic beliefs, however, there were marked differences between the two.

Kawabata was strongly influenced by Heian literature, which was compiled in the *Shin Kokin Shu* in 1206. This literature is characterized first by an almost exclusive concern with sensual pleasure and the beauty of Nature (60). Its second characteristic is the world view of Heian Buddhism—that life is suffering and death is sweet, and that animistic spirits exist and influence the living.

Kawabata's emphasis on the senses made him advocate *Shin Kankaku Ha* (new sensualism) in 1926, as opposed to the then mainstream of Japanese literature, which stressed Marxian ideology and naturalistic exposition in the tradition of modern Western writing. His emphasis on sensual gratification is represented in *Nemureru Bijo* (*Sleeping Beauties*), in which an old man wishes to sleep with sleeping beauties even though they cannot talk or have sexual intercourse. This novel also reflects the decline of Kawabata's capability for sensual gratification. He had never been strong physically; indeed, he called himself *byoki no tonya* (wholesale dealer of diseases) (61), and before he was awarded the Nobel Prize, his physical strength was extremely weak. The political campaign in which he was engaged also deprived him of much time and energy and worsened his health. His weakness, together with his old age, made it impossible for him to enjoy beauty and to gratify sensual desires. Consequently, life lost its meaning for him, and death became preferable to mere biological existence.

The pessimistic philosophy of Heian Buddhism informs the main theme of *Snow Country*: Komako loves Shimamura, but his feeling toward her is never clear. She fears that her love will never be rewarded, and will only leave her in a desperate loneliness. Despite the fear, she cannot but wait for him. This is Kawabata's view of life; there is no hope that a man can control his future. This pessimism led to his denial of any hope for modern Japan and to his intense hostility against progressive politicians (62). Given this pessimism, when Kawabata faced lasting frustration, his will to live probably was overwhelmed by a wish for eternal rest.

Kawabata's mysticism was another important cause of his suicide. He believed in the existence and influence of spirits separated from the human body (63). Once when he was being massaged, he suddenly rose and said, "Welcome, Nichiren-same." Nichiren founded the Nichiren Sect of Buddhism in 1253. At another time, when he was also being massaged, he again rose and said, "Mishima-kun! Did you come to help me campaign?" (64). Mishima had been dead for more than a year then. Kawabata believed in reincarnation, which he considered the "richest dream" and the "most beautiful lyric of life" (65). His mysticism was expressed in his sense of beauty, which was best realized in the world of phantoms between life and death. In his mind, there was little difference between this life and the afterlife; life and death were two phases of the same phenomenon. Recalling that Kawabata often disappeared from his friends for long times, and that after a while he would send them notes to come and get him, Kon theorizes that Kawabata might have left the world in much the same way as he took off on a trip (66).

In contrast to Kawabata, who was attracted by Heian literature, characterized by sensual gratification and pessimism,

Mishima was attracted by Wang-Yang-min's philosophy of spiritualism and activism. This philosophy states that the ultimate significance of life lies in attaining the "great nothingness." In order to attain it, it is necessary to reject one's self for a great cause. Although Mishima maintained that Wang-Yang-min's "great-nothingness" was the root of his philosophy (67), there was a great difference between the two.

The "great nothingness" is, as Mishima himself said, "the root of creation and the fundamental truth beyond good and bad." When a person attains it, his action reaches "justice beyond life and death" (68). Heihachiro Oshio, a scholar of the Wang-Yang-min school, and one of a few scholars whom Mishima respected, demanded in 1837, a time of terrible famine, that the government open its storehouses to the starving people of Osaka. The government officials refused, and in desperation Oshio and his men broke open the storehouses. "This triumph was short lived....He dismissed his followers and killed himself" (69). In Oshio's mind, the "great nothingness" was the root of the justice for which he died. On the other hand, the "great nothingness" for Mishima was not the root of justice, but an action characterized by "solitude, tension, and tragic resolution" (70). The more apparently meaningless the action, the better, because it was "purer and more unique" (71). It was a moment of ecstasy that Mishima wanted; it was really his own ultimate satisfaction. His activism, thus, seems to be closer to *koodo maibotsu shugi* (the principle of merging oneself in action for the purpose of reducing tension) than to Wang-Yang-min's revolutionary ideology. His desire for ecstasy was best satisfied by a suicide in the most dramatic possible situation.

ATTITUDE TOWARD SOCIAL RESOURCES

Generally the more positive the perception that social resources may be used for problem solving, the greater immunity to suicide. If the person in trouble feels that other people, expecially his significant others, are helpful, the feeling functions as a deterrent to suicide. Japanese people are generally reluctant to help anyone in trouble for fear of becoming obliged to the victim (72). One of my subjects explained this reluctance or indifference in terms of three characteristics: (1) *shimaguni konjo* (insular mentality), the way that people fight against each other for even a little gain; (2) the inhuman exploitation of inferiors in Japanese capitalism, with people concerned only with their own personal profit at the expense of the weaker; and (3) *hooken-sei* (feudalism, which in Japan means everything opposed to modernity), which stifles individuality, and deprives the individual of the capacity to solve his own problems, of confidence in his own development, and of potential for self-expression.

The mistrust of other people was shared by Mishima, as shown by his belief that he had been repeatedly betrayed by his seniors and friends. Even when Fujiko, in *Kyoko no Ie*, was desperately lonely, she did not approach other Japanese in New York, because they were "enemies." Kawabata did not make any specific statements about people's attitudes toward others in trouble; however, none of the protagonists in his novels and stories is supported warmly by his relatives, friends, or society. Most of them are lonely figures, who do not count on other people's good will, and this probably suggests Kawabata's own attitude. He was a fatalist, believing that any human endeavor could not change fate, and he denounced human efforts to solve problems, frequently using the word *toro*, which means that human endeavor is useless. *Toro* is used at least a dozen times in his short novel, *Snow Country*.

SUMMARY

A man is like no other men, as well as like all other, and also like some other men (73). His idiosyncracy comes from the emotional meaning which he gives to an environmental situation. The emotional meaning is produced by his personal situation, that continuing series of interactions between his personality and his environmental situations.

Sociological analyses of suicide which focus solely on environmental situation are not applicable to individual cases, because they ignore the importance of the personal situation. Durkheim himself was aware of the importance of personality and psychological factors, and used them frequently in his analysis of suicide. However, an application of Durkheim's behavioral indicators to the suicides of Yasunari Kawabata, the 1968 Nobel Prize winner for literature, and Yukio Mishima, a candidate for the same prize in the same year, described both suicides as egoistic, although there were great differences between them. It seems apparent, therefore, that any explanation of a particular suicide must be based on a consideration of the individual's personal situation as a product of the interaction between his personality and his immediate environment; it is not simply a matter of either environment or psychology. For every suicide shares basic needs with all other human beings, as well as ideals common to the other members of his culture; and both must be taken into account.

REFERENCES

1. Douglass, Jack D. *The Social Meaning of Suicide.* Princeton: Princeton U. Press, 1967; Breed, Warren. "Five Components of A Basic Suicide Syndrome," *Life-Threatening Behavior,* 2 (Spring, 1972).

2. Durkheim, Emile. *Suicide.* Trans. by J.A. Spaulding & G.Simpson. Glencoe, Ill.: Free Press, 1951. 211-53.

3. *Ibid.,* Chap. 6.

4. *Ibid.,* 212.

5. Iga, M. "A Concept of Anomie and Suicide of Japanese College Students," *Life-Threatening Behavior,* 1 (Winter, 1971).

6. Weissman, Phillip. "The Suicide of Hemingway and Mishima: A Study of the Narcissistic Ego Idea." Unpublished, undated manuscript.

7. Hirano, Ken. "Bungei Jihoka: Kawabata Yasunari" (Yasunari Kawabata: Commentator on Current Literature), *Sekai* (World) (June, 1972), 285; Seidenstecker, E.G., "Kawabata Yasunari to tomo ni Hitotsu no Jidai wa Satta" (With Yasunari Kawabata an Era is Gone), *Chuuo Kooron* (June, 1972), 347.

8. *The Shuukan Gendai,* Dec. 12. 1970; *The Bungei Shunju,* Feb., 1971.

9. Mizutsu, Kenji. *Mishima Yukio no Higeki* (Tragedy of Yukio Mishima). Tokyo: Toshi Shuppan-sha, 1971. 39.

10. *Ibid.,* 38.

11. *Ibid.,* 118.

12. Shabicoff, P., "Yukio Mishima." *New York Times Magazine,* August 2, 1970.

13. *Shuukan Gendai. op. cit.,* 87.

14. Mizutsu, *op. cit.,* 97.

15. *Shuukan Gendai, op. cit.*

16. Mitzutsu. *op. cit.,* 99.

17. Vidal, Gore. "Mr. Japan: Review of *Sun and Steel* by Yukio Mishima," *The New York Times Book Review,* June 17, 1971.

18. Mizutsu. *op. cit.,* 88.

19. *Ibid.,* 70.

20. *Shuukan Gendai. op. cit.,* 151.

21. Quigley, H.S. and Turner, J.E. *The New Japan.* U. of Minn. Press, 1956, 11.

22. Riesman, D. and Riesman E., *Conversations in Japan.* New York: Basic Books, 1967. 18.

23. Ben Dasan, Isaiah. *Nihon-jin to Yudaya-jin* (The Japanese and the Jew). Tokyo: Kadokawa Shoten, 1971. 114-15.

24. Doi, Takeo. *"Giri-Ninjo:* An Interpretation." Read at the Bermuda Conference of Mental Health, Jan. 21-26, 1963.

25. Ben Dasan, I., "Asahi Shimbun no Gomen Nasai" (Apology in the Asahi Press), *Shokun* (Gentlemen) Jan., 1972, 44.

26. Mita, Soosuke. *Gendai Nihon no Seishin Koozo* (Psychological Structure of Modern Japan). Tokyo: Koobundo, 1967. 156.

27. Kawashima, Takeyoshi. *Nihon Shakai no Kazoku-teki Koosei* (Familistic Composition of Japanese Society). Tokyo: Gakusei Shobo, 1948.

28. Iga, M., "Studies of Social Problems by Japanese Scholars," *Rice University Studies* 56 (Fall, 1970).

29. Nakamura, Shinichiro. "Kyomu o Mitsumeru Bigaku" (Aesthetics Gazing at a Vacuum), *The Asahi Journal,* April 28, 1972, 23.

30. Nakamura, Hajime. *Ways of Thinking of Eastern Peoples.* Honolulu, Hawaii: East-West Center Press, 1964.

31. Ben Dasan, 1971. 25, 130.

32. Kawabata, Y., *Snow Country.* Trans. by Seidenstecker. New York: Berkeley Medallion, 1972.

33. ———, *Complete Works of Yasunari Kawabata.* Tokyo: Shincho-sha, 1970. 23.

34. *Ibid.,* 116.

35. Kon, Tooko. "Honto no Jisatsu o Shita Otoko" (The Man who Committed a Real Suicide), *The Bungei Shunju.* June, 1972, 346.

36. *Bungei Shunju, op. cit.,* 221.

37. *Ibid.,* 223.

38. Kawabata, 1970. 588.

39. Ooka, Shoohei. "Ikinokotta Monoe no Shoogen" Testimony to Those Who Remain Alive), *The Bungei Shunju.* Feb., 1971, 110.

40. Muramatsu, Tsuyoshi. "Watashi wa Sore o Yochi Shite Ita" (I Foresaw It), *Shuukan Gendai.* Dec. 12, 1970, 53.

41. Mizutsu, *op. cit.,* 70.

42. Keene, Donald. "Mizukara o Horoboshita Sakka no Keifu" (Lineage of the Writers Who Destroyed Themselves), *The Sunday Mainichi.* March 19, 1972, 58.

43. Mishima, Yukio. *Kyoko no Ie* (Kyoko's House). Tokyo: Shincho-Sha, 1959. 459.

44. *Ibid.,* 500.

45. *Ibid.,* 509.

46. Ringel, Erwin. "Suicide Prevention—Psychopathological Facts and Its Treatment," *VITA,* 4 (June, 1968), 10-16.

47. Funkunaga, Takehiko. "Kaisetsu" (Interpretation), in Kawabata, 1970,702.

48. Nakamura, S., *op. cit.,* 23.

49. Fukushima, Akira. "Mishima Yukio no Naiteki Sekai" (Inner World of Yukio Mishima), *Gendai no Esupuri* (The Spirit of Today). July,1971, 258.

50. *Bungei Shunju,* Feb., 1971, 238.

51. Mizutsu, *op. cit.,* 125.

52. Horney, Karen. *New Ways in Psychoanalysis.* New York: W.W. Norton & Company, 1939. 88.

53. Mizutsu, *op. cit.,* 57, 58.

54. Seidenstecker, *op. cit.,* 347.

55. Nakamura, S., *op. cit.,* 23.

56. Weissman, *op. cit.*

57. Ishikawa, Hiroyoshi. *Nihonjin no Shakai Shinri* (Social Psychology of Japanese People). Tokyo: Sanichi Shobo, 1965. 39-41.

58. Nakamura, S., *op. cit.*

59. Ben Dasan, 1971. 134.

60. Yamada, Munemutsu. "Yuki-Tsuki-Hana no Shiso" (Ideology of Snow-Moon-Flower), *The Asahi Journal,* April 28, 1972. 18-22.

61. Kon, *op. cit.,* 249.

62. Seidenstecker, *op. cit.,* 347.

63. Kon, *op. cit.,* 284.

64. *Ibid.,* 249.

65. Kawabata, 1970. 599.

66. Kon, *op, cit.,* 252.

67. Mishima, Yukio. "Kakumie Tetsugaku to Shite no Yoomei'gaku" (Wang-Yang-min Philosophy as a Revolutionary Ideology), in Mishima, *Koodo-gaku Nyuumon* (Introduction to the Study of Action). Tokyo: Bungei Shunju-Sha, 1970. 217.

68. *Ibid.,* 216.

69. Keene, Donald. "Mishima," *The New York Times Book Review,* Jan. 3, Jan. 3, 1971. 5.

70.   Mishima, 1970. 56

71.   Muramatsu, *op. cit.,* 54.

72.   Trumbull, Robert, "Japan Turns Against the Gyangu," *The New York Times Magazine.* Nov. 30, 1958, 74; Ohara, Kenshiro. *Nihon no Jisatsu* (Suicide in Japan). Tokyo: Seishin Shobo, 1965. 246.

73.   Kluckhohn, Murray & Schneider. *Personality in Nature, Society and Culture.* New York: A Knopf, 1954. 53.

VII
Suicide and Women

BARBARA SUTER

THE MOST STRIKING SEX DIFFERENCE IN SUICIDAL BEHAVIOR IS the ratio of completed to attempted suicides. Males complete suicide about three times more frequently than females, while females attempt suicide two to three times more often than males (22). Moreover, suicide attempts are six to ten times more frequent than completions (61). Although these differential rates have been used to evaluate the relative mental health status of males and females, a simple comparison of the suicidal behavior of the sexes leads to confusion. For example, as Gove (28) pointed out, if completed suicide is an index of psychological distress, then men are more distressed than women. On the other hand, if suicide attempts are taken as a sign of distress, then we may conclude that women are more distressed than men, which is consistent with higher rates of mental illness among women (13, 29).

It is not the intent of this paper to enter into a competition about who is worse off in our society, males or females. Rather, the purpose is to focus on the distress of females as it is manifested in suicidal behavior, including attempts, threats, and gestures, as well as commits.

Suicide terminology is not always clearly defined. *Completed suicide* commonly means "the intentional taking of one's life," but *suicide attempt* is a looser term, and is used to refer to cases in which people unsuccessfully try to kill themselves (16); to cases where there is only minimal intention of dying (19); and also to cases in which there is no intention of dying (61). These last cases might more appropriately be labeled suicidal gestures. It must be recognized, however, that authors do not always specify what they mean by *suicide attempt*, probably because of the difficulty of determining the exact nature of the suicidal patient's intention. Studies which refer to suicide attempts may therefore include any of the categories delineated above, unless it is specifically stated otherwise.

A basic view of suicide taken in this paper is that it is an act of despair, an act of a person who sees no other viable options open to him/her. A suicide attempt (that is, where the person does not fully intend to die), occurs when a person is despairing about his/her own ability to cope, but still has the hope of being helped by others.

A suicide attempt, in this sense, is a particularly "feminine" act, according to society's standards, since it combines a feeling of personal helplessness with the idea of rescue by someone else. By these same social standards, a completed suicide is more "masculine," in that, if men feel hopeless, they are not "supposed" to look for outside help.

The socialization process, that is, the process by which one learns culturally approved patterns of behavior, is the focus of the following discussion, since the basic thesis of this paper is that the normal socialization process makes females vulnerable to self-destructive behavior, particularly under stress. In this context, suicide may be understood as an extreme manifestation of a generally self-destructive pattern of behavior.

I would first like to examine how a girl's learning in selected aspects of socialization—competence, identity, aggression, and sexuality—may predispose her to suicidal behavior, and then discuss women's attitudes toward themselves, in order to examine the effects of feminine socialization on the self-concept. I will then go on to investigate how social role influences suicidal behavior in three life stages: adolescence, adulthood, and middle age. I will not include old age because there is little available information about problems specific to women in this age period.

SOCIALIZATION

Sense of Competence. White (63) defined "sense of

competence" as the experience of knowing that one's own actions are effective in dealing with the environment. White & Watt (64) stressed the importance of competence to the development of self-esteem by quoting Silverberg, who stated that:

(Throughout life self-esteem has these two sources: an inner source, the degree of effectiveness of one's own activity; and an external source, the opinions of others about oneself. Both are important, but the former is the steadier and more dependable one. Unhappy and insecure is the man who, lacking an adequate inner source for self-esteem, must depend for this almost wholly upon external sources.)It is the condition seen by the psychotherapist almost universally among is patients.

To which I will add that there are many more women in therapy than men.

While it is likely that most people in our present society have difficulty achieving a sense of competence, the point here is that the socialization process tends systematically to build into women the opposite of a sense of personal mastery. Moreover, many of the abilities the female does develop are a source of conflict for her, rather than a source of strength, since these abilities may be considered unfeminine.

In infancy, of course, males are as dependent upon caretakers as are females. Mothers, however, and certainly fathers, traditionally allow and even encourage more dependent behavior in girl children (4). One way in which this dependency manifests itself in pathological form in childhood is in school phobia, in which the main dynamic is usually fear of separation from the mother. Girls have a higher incidence of school phobia than do boys, which is a reversal of the usual sex ratio of incidence of childhood psychological disorders (35).

Dependency training in the girl may be carried to the extent that she fails to achieve a real sense of personal competence. Instead of learning to do things for herself, she is taught to evoke appropriate responses from other people who will then master the environment for her. "He's a real little boy" evokes the image of an active, naughty, self-assertive, curious child who gets himself dirty and cuts his knees a lot. In the process, he is exploring his environment and learning how to deal with it. "She's a real little girl" evokes the image of a pretty, fluffy child who enjoys wearing dainty dresses which she keeps clean while she plays in a ladylike way. In the process, she is learning how to manipulate people—daddy, for example—by her cute ways. Nora, in *A Doll's House*, is a frighteningly clear picture of this model of femininity as she performs little tricks to get favors from her husband. As Dr. Goodman repeatedly tells the readers of his newspaper advice column, "Charm is the strength of woman. Strength is the charm of man."

Males are pushed to be competent and successful, which of course causes problems for them. The pressure on females, however, is more like a double bind. All children are expected to do well in school, but girls also receive a second message about never being as capable as a boy. The result is that females tend to do well in school, but in a feminine—that is, passive and docile—way. Thus, even though girls may earn higher grades than boys, their self-evaluation is such that they expect to fail, and they avoid making the effort necessary to achieve mastery on difficult tasks, thereby perpetuating their sense of incompetence. In fact, in a study of children in the first to third grades, Crandall, Katkovsky & Preston (14) found that the brighter girls had even less expectation of being successful on intellectual tasks than the average girls. As a group, the boys were not only more realistic in their expectations, but they set higher standards for themselves. Boys also felt that they, rather than fate or other people, determined their own success or failure.

This set to fail exists despite the fact that girls initially develop faster, and despite the fact that there are no significant differences in intellectual ability between girls and boys until high school (43). When girls reach adolescence they show the effects of the double message even more clearly. They become significantly less productive as students, and may even show a decrease in I.Q. Komarovsky (37) and Horner (31) both point out that a role conflict exists among female college students who fear academic achievement because it may lead to social rejection, and because it conflicts with their idea of femininity.

On college boards, males and females score about equally well on verbal aptitude, but boys score significantly higher on the quantitative index. This finding is consistent with the stereotyped notion that females are poor at math. Milton (47), however, found that females' mathematical ability improved when problems were worded in cooking and gardening terms. Perhaps women feel they are allowed to think more clearly when dealing with feminine issues.

There are many more studies which demonstrate the difficulty which females experience in developing a sense of mastery. How does a sense of competence relate to suicidal behavior?

Farber (21) stresses that a sense of competence or mastery is important to the maintenance of hope, and thus to the avoidance of despair. He states that a person may tend to suicidal behavior because of a chronically reduced sense of competence, or when a change in the environment diminishes a feeling of competence. This explanation seems especially pertinent to the female who is likely to have a shaky sense of competence to begin with, and then may be faced with a particularly stressful situation. Her usual method of coping by influencing others to help her may, perhaps, have failed, or she may be too angry to appeal to others; and thus she turns to some desperate act of self-destructive behavior.

Farber also points out that some people feel competent only when supported by someone they see as stronger than themselves. This appears to be an important factor in the suicidal behavior of widows. That is, since women are conditioned to need men to the point that they feel they cannot cope without them, it is not surprising that widows outnumber widowers in incidence of *completed* suicides, which is a reversal of the usual sex ratio.

Seligman (57) links lack of a sense of mastery to depression and suicidal behavior. He states that a life experience which has not allowed a person to develop a sense of mastery, a sense that his/her actions have a direct effect on the environment, may produce a vulnerability to depression. Since women are more likely than men to have a deficient sense of mastery, it is consistent with Seligman's ideas that depression is a feminine disorder—that is, that there is a significantly higher rate of depression among females than among males (13).

An examination of some of the primary symptoms of depression shows why it is more common among women: low self-esteem, feelings of rejection, inability to express aggression overtly, physical and mental inertia, and crying spells. These symptoms of depression are extreme forms of feelings and behavior which are typically found in many women, and which in milder form are considered feminine. What, then, accounts for the intensification of these behaviors to the point where the woman is labeled "depressed?" Depression is frequently explained as a reaction to loss. In psychoanalytic theory, the loss is that of an ambivalently loved person, and the depression represents anger toward the introjected love object. Other theories define loss in various ways—loss of role, meaning, self-esteem, and so on. The importance of role loss in middle-aged depression will be discussed later in this paper, but other contributory factors to depression are relevant to the understanding of females of any age. Chesler (13) contends that female children are not as accepted by their mothers as male children are, and that this maternal rejection or sense of loss makes them more vulnerable to depression than males. Although studies do show that women prefer to have male children (24), it is difficult to determine whether female children are actually subjected to more maternal rejection.

Chesler's view of the foundations of depression in females is an interesting one, and it is consistent with Pearce and Newton's (49) theory of depression. They describe four basic elements of the depressive syndrome: flattening of intense emotion, subjective discouragement, intense inertia, and preoccupation with suicide. They state that (although some degree of depression is unavoidable in our society, its extent depends on how "alive" one is allowed to be in early life. That is, they see depression as the result of the mother's being in conflict, consciously or unconsciously, about wanting her child to survive. The child responds to the mother's ambivalence by toning down his or her aliveness.) Suicidal behavior, then, is seen as acquiescence to mother's wish that one be "not alive." Pearce and Newton do not compare differential maternal rejection of male and female children. But in a baby, "aliveness" has to be defined largely in terms of motor activity—curiosity, exploratory behavior, manipulation of objects in the environment; and such active behavior is considered more appropriate in boys than in girls. Goldberg and Lewis (26) have shown that differential treatment of the sexes begins in infancy. Thus, in the sense of toning down of sensory experience, aliveness is less tolerated in females, probably beginning in infancy.

Sense of Identity. Striving to achieve a personal sense of identity and autonomy is a major aspect of life in our society. (The process of socialization limits the degree to which a female can achieve this goal, however, since it conceptualizes her basic role as that of an object whose major function is to nurture, to service, to be a helper.) Since her major goal in life is to be chosen by a man and to become his helpmate, it is not surprising that, from infancy, a girl's looks are emphasized, as well as the importance of her pleasing others, and putting others' needs before her own. Thus, to the degree that their identity is continually dependent on others' evaluations, women lack a well-developed sense of autonomy.

Douvan and Adelson (18) report that when they are only fourteen, boys think about what they are going to do in the world. Girls who identify with the traditional female role, however, are at the same age more vague and unrealistic about the future. The authors found that even those girls who say they intend to have careers show little of the commitment required by their future goal. (Instead, girls are preoccupied with personal attractiveness and popularity with boys.) They conclude that these concerns are functional to the adult feminine role of wife and mother, but they also state that the sense of continuity—that is, the feeling of self-sameness between what one is and what one seems to be to others—which Erikson considers central to identity formation, is specifically obstructed by girls' involvement in the dating ritual.

A concise way of formulating the major sex difference in identity formation is that boys *do* and girls *are*. That is, boys are trained to assert themselves, to achieve, to make an impact on the environment. Girls, however, are expected only to fulfill their biological feminity, which is most appropriately done through sexual and emotional receptivity. In 1792, Mary Wollstonecraft wrote, in *A Vindication of the Rights of Women*: "Taught from infancy that beauty is woman's sceptre, *the mind shapes itself to the body,* and roaming round its gilt cage, only seeks to adorn its prison." Two hundred years later, Rapone described identity in the female as "the body is the role."

In Erikson's (20) scheme, identity formation occurs before the ability to have intimate relationships. Yet, traditionally, women's identity is largely defined through the man she marries. Thus, not surprisingly, Erikson states that he is frequently asked if a female can have an identity before marriage. His response is:

> Granted that something in the young woman's identity must keep itself open for the peculiarities of the man to be joined and of the children to be brought up, I think that much of a young woman's identity is already defined in *her kind of attractiveness* and in the selective nature of *her search for the man* (or men) by whom she wishes to be sought (my italics).

Erikson points out that his statement refers to the psychosexual aspect of identity, and that females can develop other aspects of their identity. The evidence (18, 3) however, indicates that females find it difficult to develop other areas, and that their identity continues to be formed mainly around the psychosexual aspect. That is, the female's sense of identity is shaped around her sense of attractiveness to another—first in anticipation of the kind of man who will choose her, and then through her relationship with him. Feminists sometime refer to this process as the "Sleeping Beauty" syndrome. As in the fairy tale, women's potentiality (her sexuality) lies dormant, waiting to be activated by the man who will insure that she will live happily ever after.

Females thus are brought up to believe that their self-worth depends on catching a desirable man. Yet they are criticized for being competitive and catty to each other, for not being capable of the kind of friendship men are able to have with each other. It is considered the norm for women to have a limited sense of autonomy. Yet they are criticized for being hysterical, for falling apart in a crisis, for not being able to think for themselves. And they are taught to believe that their self-worth depends on their physical and social attractiveness. Yet they are criticized for being oversensitive to criticism, and for being vain, narcissistic, and insecure about their looks.

It is interesting that writers on suicide (17, 38) hypothesize that women may use less violent methods of committing suicide than men do because they are more concerned about what happens to their bodies even after death, and don't want to disfigure themselves. Less violent methods like drug overdose also tend to be less lethal then methods like shooting oneself, in that they provide more chance for discovery and rescue.

In addition to the self-hatred, poor sense of competence, and overdependency that I have already related to suicidal behavior, the lack of autonomy—the female "identity as object"—also produces rage toward the "controller." That is, the overdependence on the other leads to rage—rage toward the self for being in the dependent position, and rage toward other persons who have the power. However, this rage is generally repressed and suppressed, since it is dangerous to express it directly toward the person one is so dependent on. Woman who live in this situation may thus engage in suicidal behavior to express rage at their own ineffectualness, as well as toward the person who controls them. Many writers stress hostility as a major motive in suicidal behavior. Menninger (46), for example, cites the "wish to kill" (hostility directed toward the other), and the "wish to be killed" (hostility directed toward the self) as two major motives for committing suicide.

Aggression. There is a great deal of research evidence to support the claim that males have an inherently higher level of aggression than females (3). Whether or not that is true is not crucial here. The important point is that *whatever* level of aggression women have, they must inhibit its overt expression much more than men do.

One of the results of the inhibition of aggression in females is that they express anger more indirectly than males—in catty gossip, which can be more painful and have more lasting effects than a masculine fist fight. Fighting between two boys is usually viewed as a fair way to settle a dispute. Fighting between two girls is viewed as disgraceful and unnatural. Females of any age who express anger directly, even verbally, are frequently described as "bitches"; at best, they are "difficult."

Lester and Lester (38) point out that since the pressure to inhibit anger is so strong in women, their aggression may be repressed before it reaches consciousness. Woman's aggression may also be turned toward the self, and thus lead to suicidal behavior, since suicide is the most extreme form of directing anger inward. Moreover, since women also develop stronger affiliative needs, the combination of expressing aggression through self-destructive behavior, and needing to gain contact with people may account for the high rate of suicidal attempts among women. Completion of suicide would, of course, satisfy only the expression of anger.

Other data dealing with suicidal behavior among minority groups, particularly American Indians (38), is pertinent here, because the parallel between minority groups and women has frequently been made by social critics. Certain characteristics stemming from the oppression inherent in minority status make these groups susceptible to suicidal behavior. These characteristics, which are also typical of women, are low self-esteem and self-hatred, which, combined with the cultural inhibition against the expression of aggression, may lead to self-destructive behavior.

Self-assertion is one form of positive aggression, and means making one's needs, beliefs, or ideas known in any given situation. Self-assertion is the opposite of yielding to others simply from pressure to do so. Self-assertive behavior is culturally inhibited in females, for it is not consistent with the main focus of socialization, which is to produce social servicers and nurturers, who are expected to consistently, and uncomplainingly, put others' needs before their own. Indeed, there is often little recognition that women have any needs other than to nurture.

Even if a woman wants to assert herself, certain learned factors interfere. Assertion requires some confidence in the validity of one's own thoughts, feelings, or perceptions. Females, however, are not socialized to have that kind of self-confidence, as has been demonstrated in studies of women's self-concepts. Another illustration of their difficulty with self-assertion is Crutchfield's finding (15) that more women than men yield to group pressure. Clearly, it would be difficult for a woman to continue to assert the rightness of her judgment against group pressure if she has little confidence in her own perceptions. Interestingly, Crutchfield found that the type of woman who does not yield to group pressure is one who rejects the stereotyped conception of femininity.

Assertion also requires risk-taking ability, since it may evoke disapproval, rejection, or anger in the other person. Interpersonal dependency makes such risk-taking difficult, and for some women, impossible.

The emotional effects of the inability to assert oneself are familiar: self-hatred for one's own powerlessness, and hatred toward the intimidating other. Suicide behavior is a way of punishing the self, expressing anger toward others, and asserting one's needs to others, albeit maladaptively. Bender and Schilder (9) found that one reason children make suicide attempts is to assert their independence. It seems the same motivation holds true for some women. The suicide attempt may be the only way they feel they can assert their needs as individuals. Stengel's view (61) of the female who attempts suicide without the intention to die is pertinent here. He suggests that since other means of pressure are not as available to them as they are to men, women may use suicide attempts as a means of manipulating their environment. It's as if the only way such a person can make her needs known is by making herself even more of a victim.

Sexuality. Aspects of sexuality have been specifically linked to suicidal behavior in adolescence. Two are pertinent here—menstruation and masochism.

Studies indicate (38) that women may be more prone toward suicidal behavior at particular stages of the menstrual cycle—during ovulation, at the time just prior to menstruation, and the bleeding phase. One way of interpreting these data is to assume that hormonal changes during the menstrual cycle affect women's moods to the point where they engage in suicidal behavior. Certainly, hormonal changes may affect one's emotional state; but personality and sociocultural factors also significantly determine the degree and the manner in which a woman's mood is affected by the menstrual cycle. Paige (48), for example, found that a woman's acceptance of her religion's attitude toward menstruation was significantly related to whether or not she suffered from menstrual blues, depression, irritability, and tension. Paige also found that it is the traditionally feminine woman, not the career-oriented, ambitious type who is more likely to suffer from severe menstrual symptoms. A woman reacts emotionally to menstruation if she believes that her reproductive ability defines her feminity, and thus her identity. This view is prevalent in our society, in which any role for women but motherhood is considered second-best.

Thus, while women may be more likely to engage in suicidal behavior during certain stages of the menstrual cycle, we must ask to what extent their emotional response to menstruation is due to hormonal changes, and to what extent to the internalization of cultural attitudes. The negative quality of our attitudes to menstruation is reflected in the way we refer to it as "the sickness," and "the curse"; it is considered unclean and shameful, and proof that women are emotionally unstable and unreliable. A particularly important area for research is the relationship of suicidal behavior to the onset of puberty, since that may be the point at which menstruation has its most powerful impact on the personality.

Masochism (that is, gaining satisfaction from physical pain and psychological humiliation) is in the view of classical psychoanalysis an inevitable aspect of women's anatomical structure. The woman gains masochistic satisfaction from the discovery that she lacks a penis, from the pain of menstruation and childbirth, from the violence and humiliation of intercourse, and in general from the acceptance of her passive role.

Not all analysts accept this traditional view of women, however. Horney pointed out (32) that sociocultural factors were crucial to the understanding of feminine masochism. She stated that although masochism is not an inevitable result of feminine biology, an individual woman who may have masochistic needs of other origins may use her biological function for masochistic satisfaction.

In its most limited sense, masochism relates to sexuality, but it has also been equated with any kind of self-defeating behavior. Like de Beauvoir (17), I believe that masochism involves seeing oneself as an object, subject to the will of others. Obviously, there are degrees of masochism, ranging from extreme pathological behavior to milder forms such as the self-sacrificing, self-effacing behavior which is usually considered appropriate to the feminine role.

Instead of seeing masochism as an inevitable part of biology, we may view it as a response to a sadistic, controlling socialization that inculcates masochistic attitudes and behavior in order to reconcile women to their subordinate position. The problem for many women is that socialization does more than reconcile them to their role, it makes them feel unnatural and guilty if they aren't masochistic. If masochism is assumed to be part of feminine biology, then it is clearly something that woman *should* be. This point of view allows men to feel comfortable with a woman who plays a masochistic role, since it is "what her nature desires." Common stereotyped concepts about women, held by both men and women, in this regard include, "Women love to be dominated," and "All women want to be raped."

Under sufficiently severe stress, the behavior of the mildly masochistic woman may become more extreme, and manifest itself in various self-destructive behaviors, including suicide, and, more commonly, suicide attempts. Unfortunately, although the woman's suicide attempt or gesture may gain her shortlived attention, its primary effect is usually that she earns hostility and contempt, thus perpetuating her masochistic orientation. In fact, one component of a woman's motivation in a suicide attempt may be to evoke negative responses from those close to her in order to reinforce her own feelings of worthlessness.

Self-Concept of Females. In view of the socialization typical of our society, it is not suprising that females, including young children, tend to see themselves as inferior to males. The self-descriptions of females contain more socially undesirable traits than do the self-descriptions of males. In fact, male self-descriptions typically emphasize men's favorable characteristics, while females tend to emphasize women's unfavorable traits. The criterion which is usually used to judge the favorableness of a particular trait is the rating for social desirability made by a sample comparable to the group studied (42, 52). While the self-concept of women does include positive traits, such as tolerance, sensitivity, and understanding, these characteristics are not among those most highly valued by our competitive society. As Bardwick states   (5): Since the sexes are different, women are defined as not-men, and that means not good, inferior. It is important to understand that women in this culture, as members of the culture, have internalized members of the culture, have internalized these self-destructive values.

McClelland (39) points out that even on psychological tests females are defined as the opposite of males. That is, if males are strong, active, and fast, then females must be weak, passive, and slow. Given that choice, even a child knows what it's better to be. Many more girls, from age three on, want to be boys than vice-versa (53). Despite factual evidence to the contrary, girls rate boys higher on school achievement, and their opinion of girls' abilities grows progressively worse (59, 45).

Goldberg (25) documented the commonly held view that women are prejudiced against women. He presented college women with professional articles in traditionally male, female, and neutral fields. The same article was labeled as authored by John T. McKay, or Joan T. McKay. Despite the fact that the articles were identical, women rated male authors higher on style and competence. Furthermore, articles by males were rated more favorably in every field, even those traditionally considered feminine, such as nutrition.

One way of understanding how society views its members is to examine the judgments of mental health professionals, since it is they who evalutate normality. A number of psychologists (6, 44) have pointed out that it is healthier to have a flexible, rather than a rigidly stereotyped, sex-role identity. Nevertheless, Broverman (12) found that the mental health professionals they studied described males and females in culturally stereotyped ways. That is, they described a "healthy mature male" and a "healthy mature adult," sex unspecified, in similar terms. Their concept of "healthy mature female," however, differed significantly from those for men and adults. Healthy women were described as less independent, less adventurous, less aggressive, less competitive, less objective, more submissive, more easily influenced, more excitable in minor crises, more emotional, and more conceited about their appearances. And that's a description of a healthy mature adult, sex female—not women as they might be due to improper socialization, but women as they "should" be in order to be described as healthy and mature.

SUICIDAL BEHAVIOR IN ADOLESCENCE, ADULTHOOD, AND MIDDLE AGE

Adolescence. There is a sudden increase in the incidence of suicide attempts with the onset of puberty. Adolescence also marks the onset of sex differences in suicidal behavior. This is consistent with the fact that it is the developmental period in which the pressure to conform to sex-typed behavior is strongest.

The sex difference in the ratio of attempted to completed suicides is greatest in adolescence. While 12 per cent of all suicide attempts are made by adolescents, 90 per cent of these are made by females (2). Method used is another sex difference in suicidal behavior: males favor violent means, while females favor passive means. This difference, which is first seen at age fifteen, continues into old age.

In our society, adolescence is commonly viewed as a particularly stressful period, due to the simultaneous occurrence of physiological, psychological, and social changes. Such stress has been linked to suicidal behavior during this period (56). Those stressful aspects of adolescent development which are particularly relevant to the adolescent girl are sexuality, sex-role identity, and social isolation.

Several aspects of sexuality are frequently linked to suicidal behavior in adolescent girls and may be particularly stressful for females: guilt, frustration of affectional needs, erotization of death, and hysteria.

Guilt. Schrut (55) and Winn and Halla (65) have reported that guilt over sexual activity is an important factor in the suicidal behavior of some adolescent girls. That guilt is more powerful among females is not surprising, since they have traditionally not been permitted the sexual freedom of males. A recent national study (60) indicates that young adolescent girls hold to a double standard of sexual morality. According to this study, only 41 per cent of girls aged 13 to 15 agreed with this statement: "So far as sex is concerned, I think that what is morally right for boys is morally right for girls, too." Among 16 to 19 year olds, the percentage of females agreeing increased to 71 per cent.

Even if girls intellectually reject the double standard, it does not necessarily follow that they are free of guilt, since initial sexual attitudes are learned early in life from the parents. And although cultural atitudes seem to be moving in the direction of greater sexual freedom for females, attitude change occurs gradually. At the present time, the sexual behavior of males and females is judged differently. For example, we still hear girls being called "promiscuous" for behavior which is considered normal or at least acceptable in males. We still hear that girls "lose" their virginity; boys "lose" theirs less than they "take" virginity from girls.

Recent changes toward apparent sexual liberation may, in fact, increase rather than decrease sexual conflict in females. A female is now expected to be "liberated," which is frequently defined by the male as meaning she must be more readily available for his sexual pleasure. Thus, a girl may feel guilty if she does (the old morality), and guilty if she doesn't (the new morality). If she is sufficiently intimidated by modern standards, the girl who is not ready to engage in sexual activity may fear there is something "wrong" with her, that she is not feminine, or that she is frigid. Consequently, she may either withdraw socially, or engage in a great deal of sexual activity in the hope of finding the man who can "cure" her. Both of these extreme alternatives are likely to lead to further personality conflicts.

Frustration of affectional needs. When a girl engages in sexual activity, she may find that her male peers define the situation in terms of their own needs, while they neither know nor care about hers. Boys may enjoy sexual activity under conditions which the girl finds both physically and psychologically uncomfortable. She is then left with the alternatives of either pretending to enjoy herself, or explaining why she is so "inhibited." The conflict here is between males' and females' expectations of sexual activity. Females are taught to seek emotional and physical tenderness from males, while males are taught that showing gentleness and affection is "feminine." Thus, females may engage in sexual activity partly or primarily to receive affection and physical tenderness. Males, however, particularly in adolescence, tend to focus on sexuality in a limited way, since their ability to express tenderness is curtailed by their definition of it as feminine.

Erotization of death. McClelland (39) describes a type of suicidal behavior stemming from what he calls the Harlequin complex—a feeling of excitement in individuals (mostly females) who fantasize death as a lover who will seduce them and take them away. Why should this complex be more common among females? Perhaps the fact that more sexual repression and denial is demanded of females may encourage them to turn to fantasy for satisfaction of erotic needs. Moreover, the girl is trained to engage in romantic fantasies in order to prepare her for her future romantic role as a nurturant sex-object.

One need only look at the love comics which continue to be popular among adolescent girls to see the nature of the romantic fantasies they are taught to have. Such stories maintain rigid sex-role stereotypes: the female's major goal is to be chosen by a desirable male, male-female relations are characterized by possessiveness and jealousy, and female-female friendships are superficial and competitive. The main theme is that love conquers all. Girls are always being swept off their feet by sweet, tender kisses in the tradition of that symbol of femininity, Sleeping Beauty.

If romantic fantasy is encouraged in all girls, we might expect it to be particularly appealing to girls who cannot find emotional satisfaction in reality because of fear or guilt about sexual activity, unpleasant, unsatisfactory sexual experience, or lack of contact with appropriate partners. Sullivan (62) stressed the possibility of maladjustment in adolescents who use fantasy as a way to escape isolation. They may develop such strong attachments to idealized imaginary figures that they become increasingly unable to receive satisfaction from real-life companions. But although girls who experience severe difficulties adjusting to sexuality in adolescence may romanticize death as a rescuer, their fantasies are different only in degree, not form, from those of the average girl who dreams of Mr. Right who will come and take her away from all this.

Hysterical personality. Freud first described hysteria as a disorder stemming from sexual repression and fixation at the phallic stage of psychosexual development. The hysterical personality is described as emotionally unstable, overreactive, self-dramatizing, egocentric, and overdependent. In fact, the classic example of this disorder is "the hysterical female," who is seductive, emotionally shallow, overdependent, attention seeking, and impulsive.

The same characteristics which define the hysterical personality are also considered important contributory factors to suicidal behavior among adolescents. Bergstrand and Otto (10) and Jacobziner (34), for example, concluded that the high incidence of attempted suicide among adolescent girls is probably due to impulsive overreaction to stressful situations. Likewise, Gould (27) stresses that the sense of drama, narcissism, and exhibitionism of the hysterical personality are conducive to suicidal behavior.

The hysterical personality is viewed as maladaptive and pathological. Ironically, however, the descriptions of this type of personality sound uncomfortably like the usual descriptions of normal females. The description of "healthy mature female" given by clinicians in the Broverman study contains some of the same phrases used by clinicians to define the hysterical personality; "excitable in minor crises," "conceited about their appearance," "less objective," "more easily influenced," and "more emotional."

From what we know about the socialization process, it is not difficult to see why features of the hysterical personality are more common among females than males. If sexuality is repressed, at the same time that sexual attractiveness is emphasized, the result is very apt to be provocative behavior accompanied by emotional shallowness. Furthermore, since women are socially reinforced not for competence, but for being entertaining, it is not surprising that they act dramatically so as to get attention and feel important

Adolescence, then, may intensify the objectification of the girl which began in childhood. She is still expected to relate to males largely on the basis of her sexual attractiveness to them, and not with the aim of fulfilling her own sexual or affectional needs. Bardwick (3) found that many of the young women she studied reported that they engaged in sex because it was important to males. Moreover, their TAT stories contained themes of "fear of abandonment; resentment of being used as sex objects; mistrust of men and hostility toward them; guilt about sex and a need to expiate it; prostitution anxieties; and feelings of degradation." What is particularly striking about Bardwick's results is that these themes were found among normal young women, not among a clinical population. Many of the subjects, in fact, were college students.

Furthermore, certain learned patterns of behavior may lead to maladaptive ways of coping with sexual conflicts—withdrawal into fantasy, or impulsive, attention-seeking behavior. A combination of strong sexual conflicts and poor coping mechanisms may lead to suicidal behavior in adolescence.

Problems in Sex Role Identity. Difficulties in achieving an appropriate sex role identity and concern with homosexuality are also factors in suicidal behavior in adolescence (54, 67). As far as sex-role identity is concerned, we will focus here on the differences between the feminine role in childhood and adolescence, because conflicting role expectations in these two stages may lead to difficulties in establishing sex-role identity.

Before puberty, for example, there is generally more tolerance of opposite sex behavior in female than in male children (5). Some girls are allowed to be active, exploratory, competent, and to engage in sports—in short, to be tomboys. *Tomboy* is a derogatory word—she's not a girl, she's a "funny kind of boy." It is true the tomboy may gain valuable experience which many other girls do not. Severe conflicts may arise, however, if the tomboy does not become more ladylike with the onset of puberty. Adolescence is a time of strong social pressure to conform to sex-role standards; consequently, the tomboy may find herself a social misfit. She may be in conflict with her friends and family alike if she does not conform to their expectations.

Investment in intellectual achievement may also represent a barrier to achieving a feminine sex-role identity in adolescence. Some girls manage to maintain their intellectual abilities throughout childhood, but experience strong pressure to not be too smart for the boys with the onset of puberty and dating (Bardwick 5, 37). Many girls who do not give up intellectual competence then risk having their femininity questioned.

A third area of conflict which may arise during the transition from childhood to adolescence involves the girl who has had a particularly close, supportive relationship with her father before puberty. After puberty, her father's behavior toward her may suddenly change. The result may be that she experiences severe emotional rejection, which she interprets as directly related to her newly developed sexuality. It doesn't appear to be equally true that mothers reject boys at puberty, perhaps because mothers are not as threatened by their sons' sexuality.

These three discontinuities of role expectations may make it difficult for some girls to move from childhood to the achievement of a sex-role identity as a woman, for in each of them the acceptance of a feminine sex role involves a significant loss for the girl. The tomboy and the intellectual achiever are expected to give up behavior and activities which they consider natural, but which are labeled "unfeminine" by significant people in their lives. The girl whose sexual maturity leads to emotional rejection by her father also experiences a loss. Moreover, although she is expected to make the appropriate sexual identification, the message she receives from her father's behavior is that there is something "bad" about her sexuality.

Obviously, there are many other reasons why a particular girl may experience difficulty achieving feminine sex-role identity. The point here is that the transition to adolescence may involve such severe conflict and doubts about femininity that it leads some girls to suicidal behavior.

Social Isolation. Many writers on suicide (33, 55, 61) stress social isolation as an important contributory factor to suicidal behavior in adolescents. In fact, social isolation is probably an important factor in suicidal behavior even in cases in which there is a more specific precipitating cause.

The typical picture of the socially isolated suicidal girl, as drawn from the literature, is one whose progressively deteriorating relationship with her parents has left her with a sense of rejection, feelings of hostility, low self-esteem, and unfulfilled dependency needs. In adolescence, she turns to a boy friend in an attempt to fulfill her emotional needs through a romantic alliance. The word *alliance* is used deliberately, to connote that the relationship is not built on a genuine ability to relate to another individual. Rather, an alliance is built on the fear of being alone, and the need to recreate the parent-child relationship in an attempt to receive the nurturance and security which were not attained in that earlier context.

Thus, the isolated girl focuses all her energy on the relationship with a male, in the process alienating herself from whatever girl friends she has. She feels she can live only through the boyfriend. If she loses the boy, or even if the romance is threatened, she may feel that she has nothing to live for; and in her terror at being alone, she may attempt suicide. The fact that she more frequently attempts than commits suicide probably occurs because she is still looking outside herself for a solution. Perhaps she fantasizes that her boyfriend will take pity on her and return; or that maybe her family will realize her need for them. If they don't, and she survives her suicidal attempt, at least she'll have the pitiful revenge of communicating the reproachful message, "Look what you did to me."

There is an interesting parallel between this picture of the suicidal girl and the behavior of the heroine in *The Story of O,* a novel that depicts stereotyped relationships between the sexes drawn out to the pathological sadomasochistic extreme. O is the ultimate object. When her lover abandons her, she wants to die. Her objectification is so complete, however, that she does not kill herself, but instead asks his permission to die. Certain suicide attempts may likewise represent the girl's giving power over her life to another. The message is, "If you love me, you will save me. If you don't love me, I might as well die."

A crucial aspect of the process of social isolation is the girl's loss of ties to her girl friends. If she maintains strong peer relations, she is not likely to turn to suicidal behavior under stress (8). Good peer relationships are a barrier against suicidal behavior even among adolescents whose family situations are disorganized.

I would like to stress that the suicidal girl whose behavior has just been described simply exaggerates pathologically a culturally approved pattern for females; that is, the pattern that emphasizes the importance of a relationship to one male to the extent that same-sex relationships are undervalued. One common result of this pattern is that mistrust and competition among females for males prevent them from gaining emotional support from each other; for the behavior which makes a girl a popular date is alien to like-sex friendship (18).

Adulthood. My discussion of adulthood will focus on the social role of women during the decades from 1920 to 1950. Single women were not studied much during this period, in contrast to women in the more prevalent roles of wife and mother.

One commonly reported statistic is that the suicide rate is lower among married women than among single women or both married and unmarried men. The usual explanation for this differential rate is that married women have a social position of stable integration in the family setting, in contrast to single women, who are thought to be relatively more isolated, and in contrast to men who experience more stress in their roles in the world of work outside the home.

Other statistics, however, suggest that the picture is more complicated than this. First, the rate of suicide attempts is higher among married women than married men. This suggests that the married woman's social role within the family does not protect her from stress especially well. Moreover, some evidence exists that the relationship between marital status and suicide may be changing. Recent findings (29, 51) indicate that in some parts of the United States the suicide rate is higher for married than for single people of both sexes; and data from various western countries indicate that the incidence of completed suicide is increasing at a much higher rate for women, including married women, than for men. Gove (28), for example, reported that in the United States during the decade between 1952-53 and 1962-63, the suicide rate for white women increased by 49 per cent, while the rate of white men increased only by 10 per cent. The rate of nonwhite women increased by 80 per cent, while the rate of nonwhite men increased by only 33 per cent. Furthermore, in the other western industrial societies for which data were provided, the average increase for men was 1.7 per cent. Gove suggests that for all countries reporting, the disparity of rates of increase can be attributed to role changes that occur after the age of 25, when most people are married.

Suicidal behavior in married women may be due to difficulties that stem directly from the traditional role of housewife. Many writers have pointed out that the change in women's role in industrial society has involved increased stress. Gove and Tudor (29), for example, point out that women had a more meaningful and thus more satisfying role in preindustrial societies. Families were larger, housekeeping skills were more valued, and there was less distinction between work in the home and in the outside world. Today, although change has led to increased frustration and fewer rewards for women as housewives, this role is still considered natural. In fact, to some at least, it is considered the only appropriate role for women. In considering the latter view, Friedan noted, in *The Feminine Mystique,* that the role of women during the decade of the 1950s was in sharp contrast to the expectations of women in the 1930s and 1940s. She compared the heroines of stories from women's magazines in the 1950s with those from the two previous decades. The earlier heroines were more individualistic and men were attracted to them as much for their character as for their looks. A startling change, however, occurred about 1949; from then on women were consistently depicted as childlike, dependent, incapable of dealing with stress, and grateful to be taken care of by their husbands.

It follows then, according to Friedan, that since women believed they *should* find this role satisfying, any dissatisfactions had to be attributed to their own inadequacies. The symptoms of this dissatisfaction—depression, apathy, emptiness—she calls the "disease without a name." Frequently women attempted to deal with these symptoms by having more children, by compulsively redecorating their homes, by chronic pill taking, or by psychotherapy. The last remedy was usually directed at helping them adjust to their feminine role. It is possible, although speculative, to see a connection between the feminine mystique, and the beginning, in the 1950s, of the rapid rise of the suicide rate among women.

Other authors also have reported signs of psychological distress among married women. Knupfer, Clark, and Room (36) found that more married than single women reported feeling depressed, unhappy, and afraid of death. Gurin, Veroff, and Feld (30) compared the psychological health of married women and married men, and found that twice as many women felt a nervous breakdown impending. They also report that the women often blamed themselves for problems in their marriages, even when these problems were directly attributable to their husbands.

De Beauvoir asserts that in the early years of marriage women are lulled into the "illusion of fulfillment" by the newness of the roles of housewife and mother. By the time they are thirty, however, they usually become distressed by the routine of those roles, and the prospect of even emptier futures. In her criticism of this role, De Beauvoir points out that in France suicide is less common in married than in single women up to age thirty, but more common thereafter.

This concept of the illusion of fulfillment seems particularly pertinent to the suicidal behavior of black women. Not only is their suicide rate higher than white women's, but at least in the population studied by Allen (1), the peak age for completed suicides among black women in 1970 was 20-24, compared to 55-64 among white women. Since black women may not be permitted even the limited options of white women, they do not have the luxury of being lulled into the illusion of fulfillment. Thus, they may reach the point of despair earlier, and more frequently, than white women.

Bernard (11) reports the paradoxical finding that although housewives have more symptoms of psychological impairment than either single women or married men, they tend to view themselves as "happy." She suggests that perhaps housewives report themselves as happy because they are oversocialized—too closely integrated into societal norms—and they are confusing "adjustment" with "happiness." If feminine happiness means being a wife and mother, they must, by definition, be happy. Yet, oversocialized people are especially vulnerable to suicidal behavior when they suffer role loss, a common problem of the middle-aged woman.

Middle age. The housewife faces major role changes when her children are grown. The self-sacrificing woman who has devoted her life to her children is particularly vulnerable to stress at this time. These are the women whom Bart (7) calls "Supermothers."

The source of Supermother's middle-aged difficulties may lie in early conflicts of socialization. The Supermother is the stereotype of the feminine woman. She is self-sacrificing, needs to be useful to others in order to feel worth while, has difficulty dealing with her aggressive feelings, and has generally conventional attitudes.

Douvan and Adelson (18) describe "feminine" girls—those most closely identified with the traditional role—as gaining self-esteem through the nurturant role, compliant, dependent, worrying more, and being more intrapunitive than other girls. These girls are considered healthy by Douvan and Adelson, although they are potential Supermothers.

At the same time that women are taught to be feminine, they are also exposed to the strong achievement orientation of our society. As a result of the conflicting role expectations placed on the female, her need for achievement may be expressed in distorted ways. That is, she may seek a sense of accomplishment in the only areas open to her, through her husband and children, and in competition with other women in homemaking skills. Bardwick (3) asserts that anyone who doubts the importance of competition for women need only examine the behavior of hostesses. They try to outdo one another to the degree that social occasions are used less for the pleasure and enjoyment of friendship than as arenas for winning the honor of being the most envied hostess in the neighborhood.

Bart (7) reports that fulltime housewives are more likely than working wives to dominate their husbands and children in order to satisfy their needs for accomplishment and power. A housewife's self-esteem is based on her role of mother, so she overidentifies with her children and gains narcissistic gratification from them. The Supermother feels that her children cannot live without her. But she also feels they have the power to "kill" her, particularly by their moves toward independence.

Bart relates Durkheim's concepts of egoistic and anomic suicide to the problem of the empty nest. Durkheim's view is that marriage per se protects men, but not women, from egoistic suicide. He suggests, however, that children do reduce suicide risk among women, but only until they mature and leave home. Bart points out that there are few clear norms governing the relationships between a mother and her adult children. When her children leave home, her status changes dramatically, and after an extended period of being overintegrated into society through domestic and maternal roles, she is suddenly unintegrated or anomic.

Since she has devoted her life to her maternal role, the Supermother finds herself with few resources to fall back on when her status changes. She is therefore particularly vulnerable to depression and psychosomatic conditions—disorders of obsolescence.She is also likely to experience rage at being abandoned by her children, but her socialization has left her unable to express this anger directly. Thus, suicidal behavior may serve both to express despair over the loss of her only function in life, and her rage at those who have abandoned her. Since she measures her self-worth in terms of the love and concern her family pays her, a suicide gesture or attempt may also be a manipulative device to gain some comfort and attention from them.

We can as yet only speculate as to how the recent changes in conceptions of the female role, due to the interest in women's liberation, will affect women in general, and the suicidal behavior of females in particular. Although progress has been made in increasing women's options, we must remember that many women experience these changes as another double-bind situation. Not only is the current role of women diffuse, the expectations attached to it are contradictory. A middle-class woman may now be told that she can combine motherhood and a career, but she must still contend with the view that she is depriving her children of a mother. Moreover, there are few built-in societal aids to the working mother, even if her working is an economic necessity. Thus, while there have been many legal and ideological changes leading toward a more equalitarian position for women, the actual status of women has not kept pace with these changes. For many women this means that expectations have changed, but reality has not.

In a recent study of suicide statistics, Allen (1) reports that in California the current suicide rate for women is almost equal to that of men. She hypothesized that the reason the rate is rising is that women are moving outside the family and into the working arena. But we know that the role of housewife in itself leads to psychological difficulties, so it is not simply moving into the outside world of work that increases stress among women. It is more likely that trying to change in a society that is basically nonsupportive of such behavior in women leads to increased despair and higher suicide rates.

The fewer resources a woman has, the fewer the options open to her, and the more vulnerable she is to despair and suicidal behavior. An obvious implication of this statement is that there must be an increase in women's resources—that is, choice on the personal level of personality integration; the interpersonal level of family and friends; the economic level of education and job opportunities; and the social level of flexible role expectations. Increase of resources for women may be achieved through political, economic, and legal advances; however, such changes will not result in increased options for women unless there are also significant changes in socialization. Women must be allowed to develop into healthy, mature adults, sex female, rather than into self-derogating non-males. Only then will they be able to take full advantage of increased choice.

REFERENCES

I thank the group of female psychotherapists to which I belong for many insights into the psychology of women. I also express my appreciation to Frieda Kurash, John Fiscalini, and Peter Stein, for criticisms, suggestions, and encouragement.

1. Allen, N.H. Suicide in California 1960-1970. State of California Department of Public Health, 1973.

2. Balser, B.H., and Masterson, J.F. "Suicide in Adolescents," *American Journal of Psychiatry,* 116 (1959), 400-404.

3. Bardwick, J.M. "Her Body, the Battleground," *Psychology Today,*1972.

4. ———. *Psychology of Women.* New York: Harper & Row, 1971.

5. Bardwick, J.M. and Douvan, E. "Ambivalence: The Socialization of Women," in V. Gornick & B.K. Moran (Eds.) *Woman in Sexist Society: Studies in Power and Powerlessness.* New York: Signet, 1971.

6. Barron, F. *Creativity and Personal Freedom.* Princeton: Van Nostrand, 1968.

7. Bart, P.B. "Depression in Middle-aged Women," in V. Gornick & B.K. Moran (Eds.). *Woman in Sexist Society: Studies in Power and Powerlessness.* New York: Signet, 1971.

8. Barter, J.T., Swaback, D.O., and Todd, D. "Adolescent Suicide Attempts," *Archives of General Psychiatry,* 19 (1968) 523-527.

9. Bender, L.L. and Schilder, P. "Suicidal Preoccupations and Attempts in Children," *American Journal of Orthopsychiatry,* 7 (1937), 225-243.

10. Bergstrand, C.G., and Otto, U. "Suicidal Attempts in Adolescence and Childhood," *Acta Pediatrica,* 51 (1962), 17-26.

11. Bernard, J. "The Paradox of the Happy Marriage," in V. Gornick & B.K. Moran (Eds.). *Woman in Sexist society: Studies in Power and Powerlessness.* New York: Signet, 1971.

12. Broverman, I.K., Broverman, D.M., Clarkson, R.D., Rosenkrantz, P.S., and Vogel, S.R. "Sex-role Stereotypes and Clinical Judgments of Mental Health," *Journal of Consulting and Clinical Psychology,* 34 (1970),1-7.

13. Chesler, Phyllis. *Women and Madness.* New York: Doubleday, 1972.

14. Crandall, V., Katkovsky, W., and Preston, A. "Motivational and Ability Determinants of Young Children's Intellectual Achievement Behaviors," *Child Development,* 33 (1962), 643-661.

15. Crutchfield, R.S. "Conformity and Character." *American Psychologist,* 10 (1955), 191-198.

16. Douglas, J.D. *The Social Meanings of Suicide.* Princeton: Princeton University Press, 1967.

17. de Beauvoir, S. *The Second Sex.* New York: Alfred A. Knopf, 1953.

18. Douvan, E., and Adelson, J. *The Adolescent Experience.* New York: John Wiley, 1966.

19. Dublin, L.I., and Bunzel, B. *To Be or Not to Be: A Study of Suicide.* New York: Harrison Smith & Robert Haas, 1933.

20. Erikson, E. *Identity, Youth and Crisis.* New York: Norton, 1968.

21. Farber, M. *Theory of Suicide.* New York: Funk & Wagnalls, 1968.

22. Farberow, N.L., and Shneidman, E.S. (Eds.). *The Cry for Help.* New York: McGraw-Hill, 1961.

23. Friedan, B. *The Feminine Mystique.* New York: Dell, 1963.

24. Garai, J.E. "Concept of Self and Sex Identification," in Kidd, A.H., and Renoire, J.L. *Perceptual Development in Children.* New York: International Universities Press, 1966.

25. Goldberg, P. "Are Women Prejudiced against Women?" *Transaction,* 1969.

26. Goldberg, X., and Lewis, M. "Play Behavior in the Year Old Infant; Early Sex Differences," *Child Development,* 40 (1969) 21-31.

27. Gould, R.E. "Suicide Problems in Children and Adolescents," *American Journal of Psychotherapy,* 19 (1965), 228-246.

28. Gove, W.R. "Sex, Marital Status, and Suicide," *Journal of Health and Social Behavior,* 13 (1972) 204-213.

29. Gove, W.R., and Tudor, J.F. "Adult Sex Roles and Mental Illness,"in J.Huber (Ed.) *Changing Women in a Changing Society.* Chicago: University of Chicago Press, 1973.

30. Gurin, G., Veroff, J., and Feld, S. *Americans View their Mental Health: A Nationwide Interview Survey.* New York: Basic Books, 1960.

31. Horner, M.S. "Fail: Bright Women," *Psychology Today,* 1969.

32. Horney, K. "The Problem of Feminine Maschochism," in J.B. Miller (Ed.). *Psychoanalysis and Women.* Baltimore: Penguin Books, 1973.

33. Jacobs, J., and Teicher, J.D. "Broken Homes and Social Isolation in Attempted Suicide of Adolescents," *International Journal of Social Psychiatry,* 13 (1967), 139-149.

160 BARBARA SUTER

34. Jacobziner, H. "Attempted Suicides in Children," *Journal of Pediatrics,* 56 (1960), 519-525.

35. Kessler, J.W. *Psychopathology of Childhood.* Englewood Cliffs, New Jersey: Prentice-Hall, 1966.

36. Knupfer, G., Clark, W., and Room, R. "The Mental Health of the Unmarried," *American Journal of Psychiatry,* 122 (1966), 8.

37. Komarovsky, M. "Functional Analysis of Sex-roles," *American Sociological Review,* 15 (1950), 508-516.

38. Lester, G., and Lester, D. *Suicide, the Gamble with Death.* Englewood Cliffs, New Jersey: Prentice-Hall, 1971.

39. McClelland, D.C. "The Harlequin Complex," in R.W. White (Ed.), *The Study of Lives.* New York: Atherton Press, 1964.

40. ————. "Wanted: A New Self-image for Women," in R.J.Lifton (Ed.) *The Woman in America.* Boston: Beacon Press, 1967.

41. McKee, J.P., and Sherrifs, A.C. "Men's and Women's Beliefs, Ideals and Self-concepts," *American Journal of Sociology,* 64 (1959), 356-363.

42. McKee, J.P., and Sherrifs, A.C. "The Differential Evaluation of Males and Felmales," *Journal of Personality,* 25 (1957), 356-363.

43. Maccoby, E.E. "Sex Differences in Intellectual Functioning," in E.E. Maccoby (Ed.), *The Development of Sex Differences.* Stanford: Stanford University Press, 1966.

44. Maslow, A.H. *The Farther Reaches of Human Nature.* New York: Viking Press, 1971.

45. Mendelsohn, R., and Dobie, X. *Women's Self-Conception: A Block to Career Development.* Unpublished manuscript.

46. Menninger, K.A. *Man Against Himself.* New York: Harcourt, Brace, 1938.

47. Milton, G.A. "Sex Differences in Problem Solving as a Function of Role Appropriateness of the Problem Content,"*Psychological Reports,* 5(1959), 705-708.

48. Paige, K.E. "Women Learn to Sing the Menstrual Blues," in C. Tavris (Ed.), *The Femal Experience.* Del Mar, California: CRM, Inc., 1973.

49. Pearce, J., and Newton, S. *The Conditions of Human Growth.* New York: Citadel Press, 1969.

50. Rapone, A. "The Body is the Role: Sylvia Plath," in Koedt, A., Levine, E., and Rapone, A. *Radical Feminism.* New York: Quadrangle Books, 1973.

51. Rico-Velasco, J., and Mynko, L. "Suicide and Marital Status: A Changing Relationship", *Journal of Marriage and the Family* (1973), 239-244.

52. Rosenkrantz, P., Vogel, S., Bee, H., Broverman, I., and Broverman, D. "Sex Role Stereotypes and Self-concepts in College Students," *Journal of Consulting and Clinical Psychology*, 32 (1968), 287-295.

53. Rosenberg, B.G., and Sutton-Smith, B. "A Revised Conception of Masculine-Feminine Differences in Play Activities," *Journal of Genetic Psychology*, 96 (1960), 165-170.

54. Schneer, H.I., and Kay, P. "The Suicidal Adolescent," in S. Lorand and H. Schneer (Eds.), *Adolescents*. New York: Paul Hasbar, 1962.

55. Schrut, A. *Some Typical Patterns in the Behavior and Background of Female Adolescents who attempt Suicide.* Paper read at American Psychiatric Association Meetings, Detroit, May, 1967.

56. Seiden, R.H. *Suicide among Youth: A Review of the Literature, 1900-1967.* Chevy Chase, Maryland: National Clearing House for Mental Health Information, 1969.

57. Seligman, M.E.P. "Fall into Helplessness," *Psychology Today*, 7 (1973), 43-48.

58. Sheriffs, A., and McKee, J. "Qualitative Aspects of Beliefs among Men and Women," *Journal of Personality*, 26 (1957), 451-464.

59. Smith, S. "Age and Sex Differences in Children's Opinions Concerning Sex Differences," *Journal of Genetic Psychology*, 54 (1939), 17-25.

60. Sorensen, R.C. *Adolescent Sexuality in Contemporary America.* New York: World Publishing, 1973.

61. Stengel, E. *Suicide and Attempted Suicide.* Baltimore: Penguin, 1964.

62. Sullivan, H.S. *The Interpersonal Theory of Psychiatry.* New York: Norton, 1953.

63. White, R.W. "Motivation Reconsidered: The Concept of Competence," *Psychological Review*, 66 (1959), 297-333.

64. White, R.W., and Watt, N.F. *The Abnormal Personality.* New York: Ronald Press. 1973.

65. Winn, D., and Halla, R. "Observations of Children who Threaten to Kill Themselves," *Canadian Psychiatric Association Journal*, 11 (1966), 283-294.

66. Wollstonecraft, M. *A Vindication of the Rights of Women.* New York: Norton, 1967 (first published in 1792).

67. Zilboorg, G. "Considerations of Suicide with Particular Reference to that of the Young," *American Journal of Orthopsychiatry*, (1937), 15-31.

VIII
The Ethics of Suicide

THOMAS S. SZASZ

Egomet sum mihi imperator.
I am my own commander. —Plautus

IN 1967, AN EDITORIAL IN *The Journal of the American Medical Association* (1) declared that "The contemporary physician sees suicide as a manifestation of emotional illness. Rarely does he view it in a context other than that of psychiatry." It was thus implied, the emphasis being the stronger for not being articulated, that to view suicide in this way is at once scientifically accurate and morally uplifting. I shall try to show that it is neither; that, instead, this perspective on suicide is both erroneous and evil: erroneous because it treats an act as if it were a happening; and evil, because it serves to legitimize psychiatric force and fraud by justifying it as medical care and treatment.

It is difficult to find "responsible" medical or psychiatric authority today that does not regard suicide as a medical, and specifically as a mental health, problem.

Ilza Veith, the noted medical historian, declares that "...the act [of suicide] clearly represents an illness and is, in fact, the least curable of all diseases" (2). Veith, it may be noted in passing, is also the author of *Hysteria: The History of a Disease*(3).

Of course, it was not always thus. Indeed, Veith herself remarks that "It was only in the nineteenth century that suicide came to be so considered a psychiatric illness" (4).

If so, we might ask: What was discovered in the nineteenth century that required removing suicide from the category of sin or crime and placing it into that of illness? The answer is: Nothing. Suicide was not *discovered* to be a disease; it was *declared* to be one. This renaming and reclassifying as sick a whole host of behaviors formerly considered sinful or criminal is the very foundation upon which modern psychiatry rests. I have discussed and documented this process of reclassification elsewhere (5). Here it should suffice to show how it affects our views on suicide. I shall do so by citing some illustrative opinions.

Bernard R. Shochet, a psychiatrist at the University of Maryland, asserts that "...depression is a serious systemic disease, with both physiological and psychological concomitants, and suicide is a part of this syndrome" (6). This claim, as we shall see again and again, serves mainly to justify subjecting the so-called patient to involuntary psychiatric interventions, especially involuntary mental hospitalization: "If the patient's safety is in doubt, psychiatric hospitalization should be insisted on" (7).

Harvey M. Schein and Alan A. Stone, both psychiatrists at the Harvard Medical School (Stone is also a lecturer at the Harvard Law School), express the same views. "Once the patient's suicidal thoughts are shared," they write, "the therapist must take pains to make clear to the patient that he, the therapist, considers suicide to be a maladaptive action, irreversibly counter to the patient's sane interests and goals; that he, the therapist, will do everything [*sic*] he can to prevent it; and that the potential for such an action arises from the patient's illness. It is equally essential that the therapist believe in the professional stance; if he does not he should not be treating the patient within the delicate human framework of psychotherapy" (8).

It would seem to me that if the psychiatrist considers suicide a "maladaptive action," he should refrain from engaging in such action. It is not clear why the patient's placing confidence in this therapist to the extent of confiding his suicidal thoughts to him should *ipso facto* deprive the patient from being the arbiter of his own best interests. Yet this is exactly what Schein and Stone insist on. And, again the thrust of the argument is to legitimize depriving the patient of basic human freedoms—the freedom to choose his therapist and to grant or withhold consent for treatment. The therapist must insist that patient and physician—*together* [italics in the original]—communicate the suicidal potential to important figures in the environment, both professional and family....Suicidal intent must not be part of therapeutic confidentiality" (9). And further on they write: "Obviously this kind of patient must be hospitalized....The therapist must be prepared to step in with hospitalization, with security measures, and with medication...." (10).

Many other psychiatric authorities could be cited to illustrate the current unanimity on this view of suicide. And lawyers and jurists have eagerly accepted the psychiatric perspective on suicide, as they have on nearly everything else. An article in the *American Bar Association Journal* by R. E. Schulman, who is both a lawyer and a psychologist, is illustrative.

Schulman begins with the premise that "no one" could claim that suicide is a human right: "No one in contemporary Western society," he writes, "would suggest that people be allowed to commit suicide as they please without some attempt to intervene or prevent such suicides. Even if a person does not value his own life, Western society does value everyone's life" (11).

But I suggest, as others have suggested before me, precisely what Schulman claims no one would suggest. Furthermore, if Schulman chooses to believe that Western society—which includes the United States with its history of slavery, Germany with its history of National Socialism, and Russia with its history of Communism— really "values everyone's life," so be it. But to accept this assertion as true is to fly in the face of the most obvious and brutal facts of history.

Moreover, it is mischievous to put the matter as Schulman phrases it. For it is not necessarily that the would-be suicide "does not value his own life," but rather that he may no longer want to live it as he must, and may value ending it more highly than continuing it.

Schulman, however, has abandoned English for Newspeak. This is illustrated by his concluding recommendation regarding "treatment." "For those," he writes, "who complete the suicide, that should be the finis as the person clearly intended. For those unsuccessful suicides, the law should uniformly ensure that these people be brought to the attention of the appropriate helping agency. This is not to say that help should be forced upon these people but only that it should be made available...." (12)

It is sobering to see such writing in the pages of the *American Bar Association Journal*. It calls to mind what has been dubbed the Eleventh Commandment, namely: "Don't get caught!"

The amazing success of the psychiatric ideology in converting acts into happenings, moral decisions into medical diseases, is thus illustrated by the virtually unanimous acceptance, in both medical and legal circles, of suicide as an "illness" for which the "patient" is not responsible. If, then, the patient is not responsible for it, someone or something else might be. Mental hospitals and psychiatrists are thus often sued for negligence when a depressed patient commits suicide; and they are often held liable.

How deeply this psychiatric perspective on suicide has penetrated into our culture is shown by the following two cases: in the first, a woman attributed her own suicide attempt to her physician; in the second, a woman attributed her husband's suicide to his employer.

A waitress was given diet pills by a physician to help her lose weight. She then attempted suicide, failed, and sued the physician for giving her a drug that "caused" her to be emotionally upset and attempt suicide. The court held for the physician (13) But the fact remains that both parties, and the court as well, accepted the underlying thesis—which is what I reject—namely, that attempted suicide is *caused*, rather than *willed*. The physician was held not liable, not because the court believed that suicide was a voluntary act, because the plaintiff failed to show that the defendant was negligent in the treatment he prescribed.

In a similar case, the widow of a ship captain sued the shipping line for the suicide of her husband (14). She claimed that the captain leaped into the sea because "he was in the grip of an uncontrollable impulse at the time," and that the employer was responsible for this "impulse." Before the case could come to trial, the ship's doctor tried to assert the physician-patient privilege and declined to testify; the court ruled that, in a case of this type, there was no such privilege under admiralty law. I don't know whether or not the plaintiff has ultimately succeeded in her suit. But again, in any case, the proposition that suicide is an event brought about by certain antecedent *causes* rather than that it is an act motivated by certain *desires* (in this case, perhaps the ship captain's wish not to be reunited with his wife), is here enshrined in the economics, law, and semantics of a civil suit for damages.

When a person decides to take his life, and when a physician decides to frustrate him in this action, the question arises, why should the physician do so?

Conventional psychiatric wisdom answers; because the suicidal person (now called "patient" for proper emphasis) suffers from a mental illness whose symptom is his desire to kill himself. It is the physician's duty to diagnose and treat illness; *ergo*, he must prevent the "patient" from killing himself, and at the same time, must "treat" the underlying "disease" that "causes" the "patient" to wish doing away with himself. This looks like an ordinary medical diagnosis and intervention. But it is not. What is missing? Everything. This hypothetical, suicidal "patient" is not ill: he has no demonstrable bodily disorder (or if he does, it does not "cause" his suicide); he does not assume the sick role: he does not seek medical help. In short, the physician uses the rhetoric of illness and treatment to justify his forcible intervention in the life of a fellow human being—often in the face of explicit opposition from his so-called "patient."

I object to this, as I do to all involuntary psychiatric interventions, and especially involuntary mental hospitalization. I have detailed my reasons for this elsewhere, and need not repeat them here (15). For the sake of emphasis, however, let me state that I consider counseling, persuasion, psychotherapy, or any other *voluntary measure*, especially for persons troubled by their own suicidal inclinations and seeking such help, unobjectionable, and indeed generally desirable, interventions. However, physicians and psychiatrists are usually not satisfied with limiting their help to such measures—and with good reason: from such assistance the individual may gain not only the desire to live, but also the strength to die.

But we still have not answered the question posed above, namely, Why should a physician frustrate an individual from killing himself? Some might answer, because the physician values the patient's life, at least when the patient is suicidal, more highly than does the patient himself. Let us examine this claim. Why should the physician, often a complete stranger to the suicidal patient, value the patient's life more highly than does the patient himself? He does not do so in medical practice. Why then should he do so in psychiatric practice, which he himself insists is a form of medical practice? Let us assume that a physician is confronted with an individual suffering from diabetes or heart failure who fails to take the drugs prescribed for his illness. We know that this can happen, and we know what happens in such cases: the patient does not do as well as he might, and he may die prematurely. Yet it would be absurd for a physician to consider, much less to attempt, taking over the conduct of such a patient's life, confining him in a hospital against his will in order to treat his disease. Indeed, an attempt to do so would bring the physician into conflict with both the civil and the criminal law. For, significantly, the law recognizes the medical patient's autonomy despite the fact that, unlike the suicidal individual, he suffers from a real disease, and despite the fact that, unlike the nonexistent disease of the suicidal individual, his illness is often easily controlled by simple and safe therapeutic procedures.

Nevertheless, the threat of alleged or real suicide, or so-called dangerousness to oneself, is everywhere considered a proper ground and justification for involuntary mental hospitalization and treatment. Why should this be so?

Surely, the answer cannot be that the physician values the suicidal individual's life more highly than does that individual himself. If he really did, he could prove it, and indeed would have to prove it, by the means we usually employ to judge such matters. Here are two examples.

Because of famine, a family is starving. The parents go without food and may perish so that their children might survive. A boat is shipwrecked and is sinking. The captain goes down with the ship so that his passengers might survive.

Were the physician sincere in his claim that he values the would-be suicide's life so highly, should we not expect him to prove it by some similar act of self-sacrifice? A person may be suicidal because he has lost his money. Does the psychiatrist give him *his* money? Certainly not. Another may be suicidal because he is alone in the world. Does the psychiatrist give him *his* friendship? Certainly not.

Actually, the suicide-preventing psychiatrist does not give anything of his own to his "patient." Instead, he uses the claim that he values the suicidal individual's life more highly than that individual does himself to justify his self-serving strategies. The psychiatrist aggrandizes himself as a "suicidologist"—as if new words were enough to create new wisdoms; and he enlists the economic and police powers of the State on his own behalf—using tax monies to line his own pockets and to hire underlings to take care of his "patients," and psychiatric violence to guarantee himself a "patient" upon whom to work his medical miracles.

Having said all this, let us now articulate what is likely to be the most important reason for the profound antisuicidal bias of the medical profession. Physicians are commited to saving lives. How, then, should they react to people who are commited to throwing away their lives? It is natural for people to dislike, indeed to hate, those who challenge their basic values. This was the basis for the great religious wars of the past, and continues to be the basis for the great ideological conflicts of the present. In short, I submit that the physician reacts, perhaps unconsciously (in the sense that he does not articulate the problem in these terms), to the suicidal patient as if the patient had affronted, insulted, or attacked him. The physican strives valiantly, often at the cost of his own well-being, to save lives; and here comes a person who not only does not let the physician save him, but, *horribile dictu,* makes the physician an unwilling witness to that person's deliberate self-destruction. This is more than most physicians can take, Feeling assaulted in the very center of their spiritual identity, some take to flight, while others counterattack.

Some physicians will thus have nothing to do with suicidal patients. This explains why many people who end up killing themselves have a record of having consulted a physician, often on the very day of their suicide. I surmise that these persons go in search of help, only to discover that the physician wants nothing to do with them. And, in a sense, it is right that it should be so. I do not blame the doctors. Nor do I advocate teaching them suicide prevention, whatever that might be. I contend that because physicians have a relatively blind faith in their lifesaving ideology—which, moreover, they often need to carry them through their daily work—they are the wrong people for listening and talking to individuals, intelligently and calmly, about suicide. So much for those physicians who, in the face of the existential attack which they feel the suicidal patient launches on them, run for *their* lives. Let us now look at those who stand and fight back.

Some physicians (and other mental health professionals) declare themselves not only ready and willing to help suicidal patients who seek assistance, but all persons who are, or are alleged to be, suicidal. Since they, too, seem to perceive suicide as a threat, not just to the suicidal person's physical survival but to their own value system, they strike back and strike back hard. This explains why psychiatrists and suicidologists resort, apparently with a perfectly clear conscience, to the vilest means. They must believe that their lofty ends justify the basest means. Hence the prevalent use of force and fraud in suicide prevention. The upshot of this kind of interaction between physician and "patient" is a struggle for power. The patient is at least honest about what he wants: to gain control over his life *and* death, by being the agent of his own demise. But the psychiatrist is completely dishonest about what he wants: he claims that he only wants to help his patient, while actually he wants to gain control over the patient's life in order to save himself from having to confront his doubts about the value of his own life. Like the most ruthless tyrants throughout history, he dominates, persecutes, tortures, and even kills his victim for his own good. Suicide is medical heresy. Commitment and electroshock are the appropriate psychiatric-inquisitorial remedies for it.

In human affairs, there always lurk the twin dangers of parochialism and paternalism. In psychiatry, perhaps because psychiatrists think they are supposed to be experts on "reality," these dangers are especially great.

Like politicans, psychiatrists must often choose between being popular and being honest; and though they may strive valiantly to be both, they are not likely to succeed. And there are good reasons why this should be so. Men need rules to live by; they need authority they can respect, capable of compelling conformity to rules. Hence, institutions, even institutions ostensibly devoted to the study of human affairs, are much better at articulating rules than at analyzing them. I shall briefly illustrate the import of these remarks by citing the recent history of our attitudes toward contraception and abortion. For, like suicide, birth control and abortion are matters that touch simultaneously on religion and law as well as on medicine and psychiatry.

Though of course widely practiced (as is suicide), birth control was regarded as vaguely reprehensible until well past World War II. Indeed, only in 1965 did the Supreme Court strike down as unconstitutional a Connecticut statute against the dissemination of birth control information and devices (16).

In 1959, I polled the opinion of members of the American Psychoanalytic Association on a number of topics, some pertaining to the moral aspects of psychoanalytic practices. Among other questions, I asked; "Do you believe that birth control information should be unrestrictedly available to all persons 18 years and over?" The questionnaire, which was to be returned unsigned, was sent to 752 psychoanalysts; 430, or 56 per cent, replied. Thirty-four analysts, or 9 per cent of those responding, asserted that they did *not* believe that adult Americans should have free access to birth control information (17).

It is significant that as recently as 1964, the Committee on Human Reproduction of the American Medical Association recommended a resolution endorsing the greater availability of contraceptive information and measures, and that the House of Delegates of the Association approved this resolution (18). Until then, the American Medical Association *opposed* free access by American adults to birth control information.

The story about abortion is similar. In my 1959 poll I also asked, "Do you regard the legally restricted availability of abortion as socially desirable?" Two hundred-two, or nearly 50 per cent of the analysts who responded, *opposed* the abolition of legal restrictions on abortion. Only 7 analysts identified themselves as Roman Catholics (19).

In 1965, the year after the Committee on Human Reproduction of the American Medical Association recommended the resolution on contraception, it introduced a proposal for more "liberal" abortion laws (that is, for laws expanding the medical and psychiatric grounds for therapeutic abortions). The House of Delegates refused to approve this recommendation. Without discussion or dissent, the delegates agreed that "it is not appropriate at this time for the American Medical Association to recommend the enactment of legislation in this matter..." (20).

In 1970, after New York State removed abortion from the purview of the criminal law, the American Psychoanalytic Association issued a "Position Statement on Abortion" affirming that, "We view a therapeutic abortion as a medical procedure to be agreed upon between a patient and her physician; and one which should be removed entirely from the domain of the criminal law" (21).

The thing to do, then, is to endorse the views of the majority, while insisting that one is representing the enlightened opinions of a courageous avant-garde.

The point I am making here is one I have belabored for the past fifteen years or more—namely, that contraception and abortion, and suicide too, are moral, not medical (or psychiatric), problems.

To be sure, the abortional procedure is, as I wrote elsewhere (22), surgical; but this makes abortion no more a medical problem than the use of the electric chair makes capital punishment a problem of electrical engineering. The question is, what is abortion—murder of the fetus, or the removal of a piece of tissue from a woman's body?

Similarly, it cannot be denied that suicide, if successful, results in death. But if the suicidal act is regarded as a disease because it is the proximate cause of death, then all other acts or events—from highway traffic to avalanches, from poverty to war—that may also be the proximate causes of death would also have to be regarded as diseases. Just so, say the modern manufacturers of madness, the community psychiatrists and the epidemiologists of mental illness, who push tirelessly for a 100 per cent incidence of mental illness (23). I say, all this is malicious nonsense.

What, then, is suicide? In the West, opposition to suicide, like opposition to contraception and abortion, rests on religious grounds. According to both the Jewish and Christian religions, God created man, and man can use himself only in the ways permitted by God. Preventing conception, aborting a pregnancy, or killing oneself are, in this imagery, all sins. Each is a violation of the laws laid down by God, or by theological authorities claiming to speak in His name.

But modern man is a revolutionary. Like all revolutionaries, he likes to take away from those who have and to give to those who have not, especially himself. He has thus taken Man from God and given him to the State (with which he often identifies more than he knows). This is why the State gives and takes away so many of our rights, and why we consider this arrangement so "natural." (Hence the linguistic abomination of referring to the abolition of prohibitions, against abortion or off-track betting, as the "legalizing" of these acts.)

But this arrangement leaves suicide in a peculiar moral and philosophical limbo. For if a man's life belongs to the State (as it formerly belonged to God), then surely suicide is the taking of a life that belongs not to the taker, but to everyone else.

The dilemma this simplistic transfer from God to State (which we have indeed made) raises derives from the fundamental difference between a religious and secular world view, especially when the former entails a vivid conception of a life after death, whereas the latter does not (or even emphatically repudiates it). More particularly, the dilemma derives from the problem of how to punish successful suicide? Traditionally, the Roman Catholic Church punished it by depriving the suicide of burial in consecrated ground. As far as I know, this practice is now so rare in the United States as to be practically nonexistent. Suicides are now given a Catholic burial, as they are routinely considered having taken their lives while insane.

The modern State (with psychiatry, its secular-religious ally) has no comparable sanction to offer. Could this be one of the reasons why it punishes so severely—so very much more severely than did the Church—the *unsuccessful* suicide? For I consider the psychiatric stigmatization of people as "suicidal risks" and their incarceration in psychiatric institutions a form of punishment, and a very severe one, at that. Indeed, although I cannot support this claim with statistics I believe that accepted psychiatric methods of suicide prevention often aggravate rather than ameliorate the suicidal person's problems. As one reads of the tragic encounters with psychiatry of people like James Forrestal, Marilyn Monroe, or Ernest Hemingway, one gains the impression that they felt demeaned and deeply hurt by the psychiatric indignities inflicted on them, and that, as a result of these experiences, they were even more desperately driven to suicide. In short, I am suggesting that coerced psychiatric interventions may increase, rather than diminish, the suicidal person's desire for self-destruction.

But there is another aspect of the moral and philosophical dimensions of suicide that must be mentioned here. I refer to the growing influence of the modern idea of individualism, especially the conviction that men have certain inalienable rights. Some men have thus come to believe (or perhaps only to believe that they believe) that they have a right to life, liberty, and property. This makes for some interesting complications for the modern legal and psychiatric stand on suicide.

The individualistic position on suicide might be put thus: A man's life belongs to himself. Hence, he has a right to take his own life, that is, to commit suicide. To be sure, this view recognizes that a man may also have a moral responsibility to his family and to others, and that by killing himself he reneges on these responsibilities. But these are moral wrongs which society, in its corporate capacity as the State, cannot properly punish. Hence the State must eschew attempts to regulate such behavior by means of formal sanctions, such as criminal or mental hygiene laws.

The analogy between life and other type of property lends further support to this line of argument. Having a right to property means that a person can dispose of it, even if in so doing he injures himself and his family. A man may give away, or gamble away, his money. But, significantly, he cannot—our linguistic conventions do not allow it—be said to *steal from himself*. The concept of theft requires at least two parties: one who steals and another from whom is stolen. There is no such thing as "self-theft." The term "suicide" blurs this distinction. The etymology of this term implies that suicide is a type of homicide, one which criminal and victim are one and the same person. Indeed, when a person wants to condemn suicide he calls it "self-murder." Schulman, for example, writes, "Surely, self-murder falls within the province of the law" (24).

History does repeat itself. Until recently, psychiatrists castigated as sick and persecuted those who practiced self-abuse—that is, masturbation (25); now they castigate as sick and persecute those who practice self-murder—that is, suicide.

In my 1959 poll of members of the American Psychoanalytic Association I asked two questions about suicide. One was, "In your opinion, how often is a *successful* suicide (in contemporary Western democracies) a rational act motivated by the wish to die?" The other was the same question about "*unsuccessful* suicide." Of the 430 analysts responding, only 2, or 0.5 per cent, thought that successful suicide was "always" a rational act: and only 1 analyst, or 0.25 per cent, thought that unsuccessful suicide was! Moreover, there were only 2 more respondents who thought that successful suicide was a rational act in "over 75 per cent of the cases"; and two who thought that unsuccessful suicide was a rational act in "over 75 per cent of the cases." The overwhelming number of respondents, approximately 80 per cent for both questions, expressed the view that both successful and unsuccessful suicide is either "never" a rational act, or is so in "less than 5 per cent of all cases" (25). In short, psychoanalysts came down squarely for viewing suicidal behavior, attempted or completed, as something "irrational," that is, a symptom of mental illness.

It is upon these confused and confusing images of suicide that our contemporary psychiatric practices of suicide prevention are based. Let me now turn to a critical review of these practices.

The suicidologist has a literally schizophrenic view of the suicidal person. He sees him as two persons in one, each at war with the other. One-half of the patient wants to die; the other half wants to live. The former, says the suicidologist, is wrong; the latter is right. And he proceeds to protect the latter by restraining the former. However, since these two people are, like Siamese twins, one, he can restrain the suicidal half only by restraining the whole person.

The absurdity of this medical-psychiatric position on suicide does not end here. It ends in extolling mental health and physical survival over every other value, whose protection justifies any cost, even slavery. In regarding the desire to live as legitimate human aspiration, but not the desire to die, the suicidologist stands Patrick Henry's famous exclamation, "Give me liberty, or give me death!" on its head. In effect, he says: "Give *him* commitment, give *him* electroshock, give *him* lobotomy, give *him* life-long slavery, but *do not let him choose* death!" By so radically illegitimizing another person's (not his own!) wish to die, the suicide-preventor redefines the aspiration of the other as not an aspiration at all. The wish to die becomes something an irrational, mentally diseased being displays, or something that *happens* to the lower form of life. The result is a far-reaching infantilization and dehumanization of the suicidal person.

For example, Phillip Solomon writes that "We [physicians] must protect the patient from his own [suicidal] wishes" (27). To Edwin Schneidman, "Suicide prevention is like fire prevention..." (28).Solomon reduces the would-be suicide to the level of an unruly child, while Schneidman reduces him to the level of a tree! In short, the suicidologist uses his professional stance to illegitimize and punish the wish to die.

There is, of course, nothing new about any of this. Do-gooders have always opposed personal autonomy or self-determination. In *Amok*,written in 1931, Stefan Zweig put these words into the mouth of his protagonist: "Ah, yes 'It's one's duty to help.' That's your favorite maxim, isn't it?....Thank you for your good intentions, but

I'd rather be left to myself....So I won't trouble you to call, if you don't mind. Among the 'rights of man' there is a right which no one can take away, the right to croak when and where and how one pleases, without a 'helping hand' " (29).

But this is not the way the scientific psychiatrist and suicidologist sees the problem. He might agree (I suppose) that, in the abstract, man has the right Zweig claims for him. But, in practice, suicide (so he says) is the result of insanity, madness, mental illness. Furthermore, it makes no sense to say that one has a right to be mentally ill, especially if the illness is one that, like typhoid fever, threatens the health of other people as well. In short, the suicidologist's job is to try to convince people that being disgusted with living is a disease.

This is how Ari Kiev, director of the Cornell Program in Social Psychiatry and its suicide prevention clinic, does it. "We say [to the patient], look, you have a disease, just like the Hong Kong flu. Maybe you've got the Hong Kong depression. First, you've got to realize you are emotionally ill....Most of the patients have never admitted to themselves that they are sick...." (30)

This pseudo-medical perspective is then used to justify psychiatric deception and coercion of the crudest sorts.

Here is how, according to the *Wall Street Journal*, the Los Angeles Suicide Prevention Center operates. A man calls and says he is about to shoot himself. The worker asks for his address. The man refuses to give it. " 'If I pull it [the trigger] now I'll be dead,' he [the caller] said in a muffled voice. 'And that's what I want.' Silently but urgently, Mrs. Whitbook [the worker] had signalled a co-worker to begin tracing the call. And now she worked to keep the man talking....An agonizing 40 minutes passed. Then she heard the voice of a policemen come on the phone to say the man was safe" (31).

But surely, if this man was able to call the Suicide Prevention Center, he could have, had he wanted to, called for a policemen himself. But he did not. He was thus deceived by the Center in the "service" he got. Evidently, those who practice in this way—and such medical deception is of course time-honored—believe that the ends, at least in their cases, justify the means.

Moreover, I understand that this kind of deception is standard practice in suicide prevention centers, though it is often denied that it is. A report about the Nassau County Suicide Prevention Service corroborates the impression that when the would-be suicide does not cooperate with the suicide-prevention authorities, he is confined involuntarily. "When a caller is obviously suicidal," we are told, "a Meadowbrook ambulance is sent out immediately to pick him up" (32).

One more example of the sort of thing that goes on in the name of suicide prevention should suffice. It is a routine story from a Syracuse newspaper. The gist of it is all in one sentence. "A 28-year-old Minoa [a Syracuse suburb] man was arrested last night on a charge of violation of the Mental Health Law after police authorities said they spent two hours looking for him in a Minoa woods" (33). But why should the police look for such a man? Why not wait until he returns? These are rhetorical questions. For our answers to these questions depend on and reflect our concepts of what it means to be a human being. That is the crux of the matter.

I submit, then, that the crucial contradiction about suicide, viewed as an illness whose treatment is a medical responsibility, is that suicide is an action but is treated as if it were a happening. As I showed elsewhere, this contradiction lies at the heart of all so-called mental illnesses or psychiatric problems (34). However, it poses a particularly acute dilemma for suicide, because suicide is the only fatal "mental illness."

I should like here to restate briefly my views on the differences between diseases and desires, and show that by persisting in treating desires as diseases, we only end up treating man as a slave.

Let us take, as our paradigm case of illness, a skier who takes a bad spill and fractures an ankle. This fracture is something that has *happened* to him. He has not intended it to happen. (To be sure, he *may* have intended it; but that is another case.) Once it has happened, he will seek medical help and will cooperate with medical efforts to mend his broken bones. In short, the person and his fractured ankle are, as it were, two separate entities, the former *acting* on the latter

Let us now consider the case of the suicidal person. Such a person may also look upon his own suicidal inclination as an undesired, almost alien, impulse and seek help to combat it. If so, the ensuing arrangement between him and his psychiatrist is readily assimilated to the standard medical model of treatment. The patient actively seeks and cooperates with professional efforts to remedy his "condition." I have neither moral nor psychiatric objection to this arrangement. On the contrary, I wholly approve of it.

But as we have seen this is not the only way, nor perhaps the most important way, that the game of suicide prevention is played. It is accepted medical and psychiatric practice to treat persons for their suicidal desires against their will. And what exactly does this mean? It means something quite different from the situation to which it is often analogized, namely, the involuntary (or nonvoluntary) treatment of a bodily illness. For a fractured ankle can be set, whether or not a patient consents to its being set. That is because setting a fracture is a mechanical act on the body. But preventing suicide—suicide being the result of human desire and action—requires a *political* act on the *person.* In other words, since suicide is an exercise and expression of human freedom, it can be prevented only by curtailing human freedom. This is why deprivation of liberty becomes, in institutional psychiatry, a form of treatment.

In the final analysis, the would-be suicide is like the would-be emigrant: both want to leave where they are and move elsewhere. The suicide wants to leave life and move on to death. The emigrant wants to leave his homeland and move on to another country.

Let us take this analogy seriously; after all, it is much more faithful to the facts than is the analogy between suicide and illness. A crucial characteristic that distinguishes open from closed societies is that people are free to leave the former, but not the latter. The medical profession's stance toward suicide is thus like the Communists' toward emigration: the doctors insist that the would-be suicide survive, just as the Russians insist that the would-be emigrant stay home.

The true believer in Communism is convinced that in Russia everything belongs to the people, and everything done is done for their benefit. Anyone who would want to leave such a country must be mad—or bad. In either case, he must be prevented from leaving. Similarly, the true believer in Medicine is convinced that with modern science guarding their well-being, never before had people such opportunities for a long and healthy life. Anyone who would want to leave such a life prematurely must be mad—or bad. In either case, he must be prevented from suiciding.

In short, I submit that preventing people from killing themselves is like preventing people from leaving their homeland. Whether those who so curtail other people's liberties act with complete sincerity, or with utter cynicism, hardly matters. What matters is what happens: the abridgement of individual liberty, justified, in the case of suicide prevention, by psychiatric rhetoric; and, in the case of emigration prevention, by political rhetoric.

In language and logic we are the prisoners of our premises, just as in politics and law we are the prisoners of our rulers. Hence we had better pick them well. For if suicide is an illness because it terminates in death, and if the prevention of death by any means necessary for it is the physician's therapeutic mandate, then the proper remedy for suicide is indeed liberticide.

To sum up:

1. Suicide is a possibility inherent in the human condition. It is an exercise of the free will of the human spirit. It is an act, not a happening or an event.

2. The claim that suicide is a mental illness or the symptom of such an illness is, in view of the current legitimacy of treating mental illness involuntarily, a covert plea for legitimizing involuntary

interventions in the lives of person who are, or are said to be, suicidal. It is a grab for therapeutic power, not a plea for human dignity. The acceptance of this view on suicide helps those who promote it, not those on whose behalf it is obstensibly promoted.

3. Like any human act, suicide may be considered a sin, a crime, or a right (in the sense of its not being prohibited by either criminal or mental hygiene laws). According to the Jewish and Christian religions, suicide is a sin. Until recently, unsuccessful suicide was commonly considered an offense and a violation of the criminal law. It is now widely regarded as a mental disease and a violation of the mental hygiene laws. Of course, suicide may be defined as a sin or a crime or a mental illness, and treated accordingly. I propose that we consider the merits of defining suicide, privately undertaken, as a human right. This does not mean that suicide is a "good thing"; it means only that suicide would cease to be a justification for involuntary psychiatric interventions, and for using tax monies for the relief of problems associated with suicide.

4. Suicidology, suicide prevention centers, and the whole gamut of related activities are, in my opinion, the manifestations of one of our current fads for the manufacture of madness. This process consists of taking a basic human act that presents a moral dilemma—such as abortion, the use of drugs, homosexuality, masturbation, or suicide—and converting it into a medical problem by defining it as a mental disease or the symptom of such disease; using the authority of the medical profession to persuade as many people as possible to submit to medical (psychiatric) treatment for the disease; and enlisting the police power of the state, and using force and fraud to coerce into "treatment" all those who are, by definition, sick, but refuse to recognize it, and thus jeopardize their own or the public health and welfare.

5. Suicidology and suicide prevention centers are among the latest weapons with which the Therapeutic State wages its war on

mental illness. Those who support this war—as the true believers in institutional psychiatry do—will support the development and use of these weapons; whereas those who oppose this war—as I do—will also oppose the weapons.

6. The ideologist loves the sound of his own messianic rhetoric; the skeptic prefers the adage that actions speak louder than words. Physicians, and especially psychiatrists, ceaselessly agitate against suicide, and lock up those of their unfortunate fellow citizens whom they can accuse of suicidal proclivities. At the same time, they commit suicide in greater numbers than the members of any other professional group in the United States. To the skeptic, the pronouncements of the doctors would be more convincing if they practiced what they preached.

REFERENCES

1. "Changing Concepts of Suicide," *J.A.M.A.*, 199: 162 (Mar. 6), 1967 editorial.

2. Vieth, I. "Reflections on the Medical History of Suicide," *Modern Medicine*, August 11, 1969, 116-121.

3. Veith, I. *Hysteria, The History of a Disease*, Chicago: University of Chicago Press, 1965.

4. Veith, I. Reflections, 116.

5. Szasz, T.S. *The Myth of Mental Illness*, New York: Harper & Row, 1961; *Ideology and Insanity*, Garden City, N.Y.: Doubleday Anchor, 1970, especially Chapter 4; *The Manufacture of Madness*, New York: Harper & Row, 1970.

6. Shochet, B.R. "Recognizing the Suicidal Patient," *Modern Medicine*, May 18, 1970, 114-123.

7. *Ibid.*, 123.

8. Shein, H.M. and Stone, A.A. "Psychotherapy Designed to Detect and Treat Suicidal Potential," *Amer. J. Psychiat.*, 125 (March, 1969), 1247-51.

9. *Ibid.*, 1249.

10. *Ibid.*, 1250.

11. Schulman, R.E. "Suicide and Suicide Prevention: A Legal Analysis," *Amer. Bar Assoc. J.*, 54 (Sept., 1968), 855-62.

12. *Ibid*, 862.

13. *Fontenot v. Tracy*, Super. Ct., San Diego Co., Docket No. 309672 (Cal.,1970); cited in *The Citation*, 21 (May 1, 1970), 17-18.

14. *Reid v. Moore-McCormack Lines, Inc.*, Dist. Ct., N.Y., Docket No.69 Civ. 1259 (D.C., N.Y., Jan. 15, 1970); cited in *The Citation*, 21 (May 1, 1970), 31.

15. Szasz, T.S. *Law, Liberty, and Psychiatry*, New York: Macmillan, 1963; *Ideology and Insanity*, Chapters 9 and 12.

16. *Griswold v. Connecticut*, 381 U.S. 479 (1965).

17. Szasz, T.S. and Nemiroff, R.A.: "A Questionnaire Study of Psychoanalytic Practices and Opinions," *J. Nerv. & Ment. Dis.*, 137 (Sept., 1963), 209-21.

18. Szasz, T.S. "The Ethics of Abortion," *The Humanist*, 26 (Sept.-Oct.,1966), 147-48.

19. Szasz and Nemiroff, 214.

20. Szasz, The Ethics of Abortion, 147.

21. American Psychoanalytic Association, Position Statement on Abortion, June 25, 1970.

22. Szasz, The Ethics of Abortion, 148.

23. Szasz, *The Manufacture of Madness*, 38-39.

24. Schulman, *op. cit.*, 857.

25. Szasz, *The Manufacture of Madness*, Chapter 11.

26. Szasz and Nemiroff, 214.

27. Solomon, P.: "The Burden of Responsibility in Suicide," *J.A.M.A.*, 199 (Jan.30, 1967), 321-24.

28. Schneidman, E.S. "Preventing Suicide," *Bulletin of Suicidology*, (1968), 19-25.

29. Zweig, S. "Amok," in *The Royal Game*, New York: Viking Press, 1931.

30. Blakeslee, S. "Clinic Here Tries to Avert Suicides," *New York Times*, Feb. 9, 1969, 96.

31. Pinkerton,W. S.,Jr. "The Lethal Impulse," *Wall Street Journal*, March 6, 1969, 1.

32. "Clinic Moves to Prevent Suicides in Suburbia," *Medical World News*, July 28, 1967, 17.

33. "Minoa Man Arrested After Suicide Threat," (Syracuse) *Post-Standard*, September 29, 1969, 10.

34. Szasz, *The Myth of Mental Illness*.

Contributors

ARNOLD BERNSTEIN
City University of New York, Queens College

MEDARD BOSS
Daseinsanalytic Institute of Psychotherapy and Psychosomatics, Zurich

MAMORU IGA
California State College, Northridge

HERBERT KRAUSS
City University of New York, Hunter College

ROBERT JAY LIFTON
Yale University

BARBARA SUTER
City University of New York, Hunter College

BENJAMIN B. WOLMAN
Long Island University

Author - Subject

Index

BETWEEN SURVIVAL AND SUICIDE

Edited by Benjamin B. Wolman
Consulting Editor, Herbert Krauss

Suicide is a public health problem of great magnitude. To Camus, there was only one serious, philosophical problem—suicide. Suicide has always been and continues to be of central concern to clinical practioners, philosophers, social scientists, and universal man.

The essays in BETWEEN SURVIVAL AND SUICIDE are wideranging but clear in their intentions. Their aim is to examine the nature of suicide through the nature of man and his society. The authors are expert in their chosen fields. Bernstein, Boss, Iga, Krauss, Lifton, Suter, and Wolman provide insights and scholarship about such topics as the existential meaning of suicide, the psycho-social field in which suicide takes place, the suicide of women, and the ethics of suicide prevention. The essays balance theory with practice, describe suicidal societies and suicidal individuals.